Rethinking Behaviour Management

RESTORATIVE PRACTICES

IN CLASSROOMS

Margaret Thorsborne & David Vinegrad

Routledge
Taylor & Francis Group
LONDON AND NEW YORK

Acknowledgements

This manual was written for practitioners who have embraced notions of restorative justice as a way of doing discipline with kids, and who have realised that most of these disciplinary transactions happen at the coalface – in classrooms and playgrounds. Instruction in the following chapters is based on experimentation by those who have recognised a good idea when they see one, and adapted the philosophy and principles of restorative justice where it probably matters the most – where the teaching and learning happens.

Again, we would like to acknowledge the early work of criminal justice pioneers in New Zealand, Australia and elsewhere. Schools in these countries have also been adopting restorative approaches to behaviour management, and it is largely their efforts, commitment and downright courage that have reinforced our belief that true culture change happens where it matters most, in classrooms.

We have been assisted in these endeavours by our own colleagues in education in Australia and New Zealand. In particular we would like to mention Margaret Armstrong, an educational advisor in Melbourne, Australia, who is passionate about restorative classroom processes, and who has been a dynamo of drive and enthusiasm in this field, teaching and leading others with her experience and knowledge. We would also like to acknowledge the efforts of our colleague Stuart Newby, Head of Student Services in a busy high school in Auckland. He has done this reform movement a great service in New Zealand schools by his ongoing encouragement and support. We have received valuable feedback and support from student managers and students at primary, intermediate and secondary schools in NZ and Australia.

We'd like to thank the desktop publisher of our first edition, Edwina Carson, who was very patient with our foibles and timelines, for her terrific job and great suggestions. Thanks mate. And thanks too to Barry Alsop who, as our professional photographer, entered into the spirit of the work and captured classic moments on film.

In the wake of recent world events, our mission is more urgent. Healing damaged relationships and making things right must be the focus of our efforts if we wish for a safer world for the young people who will grow up to become our leaders. Our thanks go to those of you who also believe this to be true.

First published 2004 by Speechmark Publishing Ltd.

Published 2017 by Routledge
2 Park Square, Milton Park, Abingdon, Oxon OX14 4RN
711 Third Avenue, New York, NY 10017, USA

Routledge is an imprint of the Taylor & Francis Group, an informa business

British Library Cataloguing in Publication data
A catalogue record for this book is available from the British Library.

ISBN 9780863886881 (pbk)

Authors:
Margaret Thorsborne
Email: margthorsborne@optusnet.com.au
Web: www.thorsborne.com.au
and David Vinegrad
Email: behaviourmatters@hotmail.com

Illustrations by Adrian Osborne

Previously published in Australia by Inyahead Press.

Contents

Foreword

Margaret Thorsborne is one of the pioneers of restorative justice, particularly in schools, in the Southern hemisphere and globally. This manual represents the sifting of all the wisdom she and her colleague and co-author, David Vinegrad, have acquired over more than a decade of facilitating restorative justice processes in schools. In this Marg and David have also benefited from the wisdom of the diverse wider community of restorative justice practitioners in Australia and elsewhere. Their networks and experience have helped forge Marg and David as the master practitioners they are. In this manual fellow educationalists are presented with the opportunity to imbibe their experience.

Practical options for things facilitators can say to bring about empowerment, cooperation and restoration are presented throughout the manual. "Scripts" are controversial in the restorative justice literature. But David and Marg offer the productive middle ground of proven scripts that give new practitioners a starting framework for what to say in the face of difficult conflicts, without being prescriptive. Indeed, they argue that as practitioners acquire experience, they will encounter many unique situations where departure from the script is imperative. Draft letters, evaluation tools and practical advice on how to approach both uniquely difficult and rather standard situations equally offer frameworks that people can adapt to their own school culture.

The manual is clearly presented, taking practitioners in gentle stages through the rough realities of confronting injustices in schools. The evidence that restorative justice in schools can be effective in reducing problems like bullying and in engendering a sense of fairness and justice among all stakeholders in the educational enterprise grows stronger. In general, people are happier and more productive working in organisations where they see themselves as treated fairly. For this reason, I believe this work by Marg and David is important in a very practical way to improving educational outcomes for both children and adults.

John Braithwaite
Australian Research Council Federation Fellow
Australian National University

About this manual

This manual has been designed to complement and support the classroom conference training programme for classroom teachers. There is no substitute for the learning and engagement that occurs when participants take an active part in training simulations or practise these new techniques in a supportive environment. An essential component of our training programmes is the exchange of ideas and robust debate with workshop leaders and other participants. We hope that you will take advantage of these workshops.

We have organised the manual in a way that will be practical and useful to you.

Chapter one begins the analysis of current practice in your school and, more importantly, in your classroom. Essential themes of this chapter include a comparison between punitive and restorative practices, system needs as against the needs of people within school communities, and the values and beliefs we hold as educators about fair process, justice and the job of producing good citizens.

Chapter two unfolds the range of restorative processes that have been developed to assist classroom teachers and student managers. The chapter sets out some of the conditions for facilitating conferences and other more informal restorative processes. It also clarifies the differences between those processes designed to enhance teaching and learning and those appropriate for responding to wrongdoing.

Chapter three details the practice of conferences that enhance teaching and learning and have been found effective as a preventative measure to minimise the risk of classroom disruption. We have also detailed some different processes that are quite specific: curriculum and pedagogy focus, responding to wrongdoing, and 'no blame' scripts or dialogues.

Chapters four to six are devoted to responding effectively to wrongdoing. They are highly practical in their processes, directions and tips. Included are the step-by-step tasks needed for preparation, planning and facilitation of individual, small and large group and whole classroom conferences.

Chapter seven lists some of the most frequently asked questions fielded in training workshops, along with our answers.

The Appendix contains key documents designed to assist your delivery of a variety of processes. We have included contributions from a range of practitioners in the form of case studies and adaptations of the conference process. Tools to assist your preparation, facilitation and evaluation of your processes are also provided. There is a list of recommended readings, including relevant websites, for you to explore further these notions of restorative practices in classrooms and restorative justice in schools. We regard this manual as a work in progress. It is designed for ease of editing, so please email your feedback, suggestions and questions to us for consideration in later editions.

Good luck!

Margaret Thorsborne and David Vinegrad

We can be reached at: marg@thorsborne.com.au

and

behaviourmatters@hotmail.com

Rethinking our approaches to managing behaviour

It is likely that you already know some basic truths about the management of behaviour as it applies in the classroom setting. When students are actively engaged in the learning process with carefully planned lessons, when their learning needs are met, when curriculum is relevant, when transitions are managed effectively, when the relationships that exist between teachers and students are healthy and based on trust, tolerance and respect, when the classroom rules are explicit, fair and enforced, then class disruption rarely creates more than a blip on the radar screen of the teacher or classmates.

Life is never so simple of course, especially when the classroom environment is a complex dynamic of personalities, backgrounds, intelligences and experiences. What will also have an impact on how "business is done" between everyone in the classroom, and in the wider school, will be the explicit or implicit values of the school itself, its sense of purpose about education, its beliefs about young people and about how behaviour is best managed.

Current practice

When teachers and school management are asked, in our training programmes, about how they engage young people in the curriculum and, more broadly, the life of the school community, most are quick to

define a set of values that underpin their beliefs about the importance of lifelong learning, responsible citizenship and the importance of community. When these groups are asked about the philosophy that underpins the way they manage discipline and wrongdoing, they generally reach the conclusion that their practices are based largely on punishment. How can professionals who value such concepts as community and citizenship also value inflicting pain/inconvenience as the most effective way to change behaviour? The answer is usually "because we've always done it this way" or "because we are responding to what we think are the needs of the system or the local community".

These more punitive discipline practices often do not deliver the kinds of outcomes we are seeking: more young people doing the right thing most of the time; young people who are thoughtful about the impact of their own behaviour on others; young people who take responsibility for their actions; the development of a sense of community and connectedness. Neither do they take into account what research is beginning to show us about the development of the adolescent brain – research that indicates that during this period of development, the adolescent brain is enjoying a growth spurt, is low on serotonin levels and could be said to be extremely vulnerable to the variety of influences which young people are exposed to at this time of their lives.

It is appropriate here, then, to examine our traditional approaches to the management of wrongdoing in schools. Traditional approaches usually follow a logic based on quasi-judicial arguments: What happened? Who's to blame? What rule/law has been broken? What punishment should be applied? In a school, wrongdoing is often regarded as an offence against the institution and its rules, modelled on a philosophy of retributive justice that seeks to inflict pain on the wrongdoer.

Discipline (usually in the form of punishment) is dispensed by a designated officer in the school, such as an assistant principal, a year coordinator or a head of house, sometimes the class teacher. The sanctions, usually some sort of temporary incapacitation such as time-out, detention, the removal of privileges or suspension, are intended to teach young people, by way of deterrence, that the behaviour was inappropriate, and that there are consequences for doing the wrong thing, while protecting the safety and rights of others to learn. For most young people, who are well connected to their families and the school community, this is enough to make them think twice about doing "it" again. Occasionally, an offence is deemed so serious that a student will be permanently excluded.

This punitive approach to managing behaviour, though, focuses on the individual, rather than the context in which the behaviour occurred, and the complex dynamics that operate in schools and families that may have contributed to the incident. The focus of the pathology is on the student, rather than the system. Neither does the punishment concern itself with the impact of the behaviour on relationships, or the emotional harm done to others, or the possibility of support needed to change behaviour. A punitive approach to wrongdoing is often in stark contrast to the values and beliefs that drive much of the curriculum and pedagogical practice in the school. These place a high value on the development and maintenance of positive, healthy and respectful relationships and a supportive school environment. If we were to redefine discipline and behaviour management as relationship management, we might find a different pathway for our problem-solving. Such a path might be found in restorative justice and its range of processes and approaches.

Restorative justice

The philosophy and practice of restorative justice has much to offer those of us who are concerned with the development of well-rounded, socially and emotionally competent young people who are accountable for their behaviour and understand that there is nothing they do (or don't do) which doesn't impact on others in some way. So what do we mean by restorative justice, and what has it got to do with education?

Restorative justice requires a paradigm shift in thinking which, for some who have never questioned the effectiveness of punishment as a means to change behaviour, is a real challenge. But for others, it is a reassurance that what they've believed in and practised for years has a name, and indeed delivers outcomes that include high rates of school achievement, low rates of offending behaviour, a sense of belonging in a community and emotional literacy and competence. Put simply, restorative justice is a philosophy that has as its framework:

- Crime (and misconduct) is a fundamental violation of people and interpersonal relationships
- Violations create obligations and liabilities
- Restorative justice seeks to heal and put right the wrongs

Restorative justice is a participatory and democratic justice that focuses on the incident and not solely on the wrongdoer's behaviour. It is an approach to harmful behaviour and community conflict that sees wrongdoing as essentially a violation of people and/or property. The community conference, a well-known restorative process, formalises the bringing together of all those responsible and accountable for, and most affected by, wrongful conduct. Individually and collectively, people address the causes of the harm, the impact of the harm, on those most affected and investigate ways to make amends and to put right the wrong done. It is not new. This type of problem-solving formed the basis of Anglo-Saxon law long before the arrival of the Normans. It was part of earlier legal traditions, including Roman law. Most traditional forms of justice were based around notions of reparation and restoration. It embraces a wide range of human attributes – healing, compassion, forgiveness and mercy, as well as mediation and reconciliation – and includes sanctions where appropriate.

Restorative justice and behaviour management

So, what has this got to do with classrooms and the way we might manage the behaviour of learners? The teacher's response to problem behaviour in a classroom is usually a reflection of school policy and its underlying beliefs, as well as his/her own personal beliefs and skills about how best to challenge and change behaviour. What are the usual "problem behaviours" committed by young people in classrooms?

- Coming late to class
- Failure to complete homework
- Failure to bring appropriate materials
- Failure to complete tasks in class
- Disruption by talking/fooling around/ calling out/throwing things
- Abusing the teacher
- Swearing
- Abusing/fighting with fellow students
- Withdrawal from the learning process
- Making a mess and failing to clean up
- Theft and property damage
- Bullying and harassment of others
- Rudeness, insolence and contempt

And what are the traditional responses to these problem behaviours? Some schools will have adopted a whole-of-school practice reflecting a 'get tough' or 'zero tolerance' approach, while other schools may be in a state of constant change as 'flash in the pan' initiatives take their interest in an effort to bring about some improvement. There will sometimes be a clear set of in-class responses that will escalate to out-of-class procedures if the behaviour persists. And we all know that some teachers rely rather heavily on this latter response to minimise classroom disruption and maintain control. Typically, it becomes someone else's responsibility to fix the problem!

If these "programme" practices are consistent across classrooms, are clearly understood by all and are delivered with respect, support and fairness, likely outcomes will be, at least in the short term, positive. But again, we need to ask if the sanction has delivered an outcome for the individual and the group. Is it characterised by the building of empathy

and thoughtfulness and accountability for one's actions to those most affected by them? In what ways does traditional punishment create an opportunity to have the kind of conversations needed to explore harm done, the impact on relationships and how to make things right?

A restorative classroom, on the other hand, will be characterised by high levels of support as well as clear boundaries, where problem solving around issues is done with students.[†] The kinds of conversations that can be heard in these classrooms are about what happened, what was the thinking behind the behaviour, who had been affected and in what way. These conversations focus on fair process, responsibility and accountability, and the repair of relationships that have been damaged. We know that to change behaviour we need to provide a process to engage students in meaningful dialogue about what they are doing or not doing. This kind of meaningful dialogue always involves discussions around feelings. Our traditional sanctions are not concerned with feelings, although at a deep and often unconscious level our sanctions are sometimes driven by revenge – the need to retaliate when our authority has been challenged – which is indeed an emotional response.

> *We have come to understand that significant cultural change is possible within schools when they choose to work restoratively with young people.*

We know all too well that students spend most of their school day in groups of two or more. It is not uncommon for some teachers to believe (and fear) that students in their classes have the potential to come together in a mass to challenge or even attack them. A great deal of literature has been written on how to manage students using an individual approach, yet we mostly work with students in classes, groups and teams. Practitioners in restorative classrooms will tell you that addressing the behaviour of one or more students within the classroom community has proved to be far more effective than removing and sending the wrongdoer to the office or time-out facility to be "dealt with" by others.

We have come to understand that significant cultural change is possible within schools when

---

† Refer to Social Control Window in Ted Wachtel's *Restorative Justice in Everyday Life: Beyond the Formal Ritual.*

they choose to work restoratively with young people. Relationships between teachers and students improve when the 'heat' and 'angst' of daily human interactions is managed restoratively. Abstract lectures to invoke compliance are exchanged for concrete dialogue about behaviour, relationships and community. When students understand that restorative processes will be fair and non-punitive, they begin to cooperate with the school and take ownership and responsibility for their own behaviour. In comparison, when punitive methods are applied, students will sometimes withdraw their cooperation and admissions of involvement. It is well documented that punitive methods do not teach important lessons about pro-social behaviour. In fact, they remove the wrongdoer from the act, teach avoidance behaviours and label him/her. Students whose behaviour has been managed restoratively, however, have been observed to undergo meaningful attitudinal and behavioural change.

Discipline as fair process

"Fair" is a word that we've mentioned several times in this chapter, and it bears closer examination. Young people and their parents, as well as teachers, are far more likely to accept the umpire's decision about how a matter has been dealt with, if they have experienced the process as fair. A great deal of energy is spent by school staff developing "fair" policy and practice, without realising what they are committing themselves to. In matters of discipline, "fair" in a restorative sense is when:

- All affected parties (teachers, young people and parents, where appropriate) are engaged in the process of problem-solving and in determining what's needed to put things right
- Everyone (teachers, young people, parents) has a chance to tell their story and to be heard
- If you've done wrong, you will be given a chance to make amends and put things right
- If you are a victim, you will have a say in how to make things right
- Opportunities will be created for all parties to understand, reflect on and learn from the experience in a respectful way
- Dialogue is participative and voluntary
- The repair of relationships and community is paramount and overrides institutional imperatives
- There is a sense of collective accountability and responsibility

In summary, fair process is about engagement and empowerment. This is in direct contrast to current, traditional practice that sees discipline dispensed by a party unconnected to the incident, sanctions linked to school policy with a history and tradition underpinned by punishment, a focus on individual behaviour rather than the needs of the community affected, and processes which do not, in any way, take into account how people have been harmed, or how to repair that harm.

Review of school policy

Some schools spend inordinate amounts of time developing staff skills in curriculum and pedagogy but fail to balance this against time spent learning about and managing behaviour. If schools and teacher training institutions are to stimulate a move from authoritarianism and punishment to authoritative and restorative practice, a serious review of whole-of-school policies will be needed. A more balanced approach across these three areas has the potential to improve teaching and learning outcomes.

The following key questions could be part of regular critical review of the behaviour management component of school policy.

For the school:

- What do we believe our job is?
- What are our core values and beliefs about relationships and behaviour in our school?
- What is the purpose of our discipline system? What outcomes does it seek to achieve?
- Where do we stand on issues of justice and fairness?
- How important to us is the development of social and emotional competencies?
- Do our daily practices reflect our beliefs and values?
- How do we articulate these values and beliefs in concrete and practical ways to our students, teachers and community?
- In what ways do we evaluate our practices and measure our performance?

For the classroom teacher and student manager:

- What are the outcomes that I want to achieve from my behaviour management plan a nd strategy?
- What are my own values, attitudes and understandings about fairness and justice?

- What are the things that my students appreciate about a 'good' teacher? Am I delivering?

- How can I make sure that my students understand the expectations about behaviour and relationships in my class?

- How can I best teach thoughtfulness and empathy?

- Is what I do and how I respond supported by research and current best practice?

- How do I know if what I do is effective and appropriate?

Schools wishing to promote responsible behaviour and develop student self-discipline would do well to adopt the full range of restorative processes available. Because these processes provide fairness and equity, the reward is the building of trust, optimism and satisfaction amongst students and teachers that in turn promotes positive behaviour

and improves academic outcomes. From our experience, real compliance is achieved with students because fair process is part of the deal. The risk of retribution and re-victimisation is significantly reduced when fairness and a focus on making things right become the foundations of discipline. Students don't 'go to ground', blame others or rationalise their behaviour when fair process asks them to talk about their involvement in an incident, who has been affected, and what they need to do to right the wrongs.

This manual will guide you into the deeply satisfying and effective realms of restorative practices in classrooms, playgrounds and corridors. Our methods are practical and proven. Once you feel comfortable with the philosophy and practice of the restorative processes outlined in the next chapters, the capacity to apply these in practically any situation will be limited only by your imagination. ■

Restorative Practices in Classrooms

Restorative practices – a continuum

This chapter will describe a number of restorative processes (conferences or meetings) that can engage and empower both teacher and student in transactions around discipline. Firstly, processes for getting it right (becoming explicit) before you start, to lessen the possibility of conflict and misconduct, and secondly, how to repair the damage when difficulties arise. In addition, we have adapted the restorative approach to deal with individual, small group, whole class and even larger group (such as whole-of-year cohort) incidents. Figure 1 overleaf shows this restorative continuum.† The processes described have evolved naturally from the formal community conference and it is entirely possible that if you grasp the concept, philosophy and basic skills, there is probably nothing you cannot deal with, with a little common sense, practice, imagination and support.

We have divided the processes into two groups:

■ Proactive processes which enhance teaching and learning

■ Reactive processes used for responding to wrongdoing

Teachers who understand instinctively that healthy relationships form a strong base for productive teaching and learning, have always contrived to invest time and energy into developing and maintaining these positive relationships. There are two aspects to this kind of investment. The first is proactive. This is about setting things up in the classroom or the sports field or the auditorium, so that behavioural and relational boundaries are explicit and respectfully maintained. The most common example of this is the practice of reaching class rules collaboratively. But it is also about developing an interesting, engaging curriculum, with well-organised, well-prepared lessons. These become protective devices and serve to keep the teacher–learner, learner–learner relationships free of unnecessary conflict and distraction.

The second aspect is about our reactive responses. This is about how teachers view and respond to the inevitable hiccups that occur when things go wrong in classrooms: young people off task; lessons going awry; disruptive, harmful behaviour. Emotionally intelligent teachers know that relationships always suffer damage when these situations occur, and that for learning to occur without distraction, these disconnections must be remedied. They understand that relationships are important. They probably intuit that punishment alone does not make things right or ease the feelings of hurt, anxiety and frustration. They understand that certain types of conversations need to be had to achieve the repair of these connections. With practice, these conversations will become second nature.

---

† A similar continuum can be found in Ted Wachtel's *Restorative Justice in Everyday Life: Beyond the Formal Ritual*

History of restorative justice in schools

It might be worthwhile at this point to examine, briefly, the history of the restorative justice movement in schools. The first "formal" community conferences were convened in Australian schools in the mid-1990's. Adapted from juvenile justice processes, these were an innovation at the time, and still are in many schools. They are used specifically to deal with incidents of serious harm, such as assaults, serious victimisation, serious acts of vandalism, fights, ongoing high-level conflict, drugs, theft, environmental damage – the sorts of incidents that invariably attract suspension and exclusion. A handful of senior and middle managers and school counsellors were trained to facilitate these conferences in each school. Evaluations of these conferences in a range of school settings – elementary, intermediate and senior/high schools – provided ample evidence of the value of the process and its many advantages over traditional punitive approaches. However, what we found was that the restorative approach, reserved for serious incidents, failed to solve the myriads of low-level issues that

> *...if you grasp the concept, philosophy and basic skills, there is probably nothing you cannot deal with, with a little common sense, practice, imagination and support.*

occurred in the daily life of the school because there were very few people (particularly classroom teachers) in these schools trained to respond restoratively. And so there was a duality of approaches operating and they were mutually exclusive. It's not hard to figure out which approach prevailed in the long term! Successful models developed since then have demonstrated the necessity of filtering the training into classrooms, where low-level issues are dealt with on the spot and prevented from escalating in the next lesson or class, into the playground or beyond into the general school community. 'Restorative' teachers understand that productive lesson time needs to be free of these tensions, and that it is worth spending the time to resolve these issues instead of trying to soldier on, or indeed removing the "problem" for someone else to fix.

Figure 1 Restorative practices continuum

Classroom Conferences in the School Setting

Individual conference	Small group conference	Whole class conference	Large group conference

Group Composition

Teacher and student	Teacher and several students	Teachers and class of students	Teachers and levels/grades/ whole years

Similar Restorative Practices in Schools and the Community

Tribes based classrooms	Healing Circles	Sentencing Circles	Family Group Conference
Community Conferences	Diversionary Conferences	Restorative Justice Forums	Victim-Offender Mediation

Culture change

A school wishing to do things differently will eventually face having to make a choice between punitive and restorative approaches. In a restorative school, young people become used to relationship language, being honest about their behaviour (because they are not about to be punished), being accountable to those they've hurt because they have to face up, and seeking ways to make things right when something, however trivial, goes wrong. Emotional literacy is improved, as teachers and students become more used to speaking comfortably about their feelings. Self-reflection and self-awareness assist the development of social skills. The social curriculum becomes explicit. The classroom and the rest of the school becomes a truly safe, supportive environment. Responsibility and accountability is shared between students, teachers and school administrators. Is this what we want, or not? This explicit choice can be the beginning of a true and lasting culture change process. Implementation will be no mean feat. Bringing all staff around to this way of thinking and doing is nothing short of a complete "retooling", and of course needs, like any large-scale change, visionary leadership, careful planning for long-term change, a willingness to take some risks, and ongoing support with quality professional development and coaching. Some schools manage this more readily than others. But if you are reading this manual, and are stimulated by the content, and you work in a school, you may find the answers you're seeking here in order to make a start and a real difference.

Restorative protocols

Central to these restorative processes are a number of protocols:

1. The meetings/conferences are conducted in a circle[†]

2. A device called a "talking stick"[††] which can be anything from a feather or carved piece of wood to a rolled-up wad of paper is passed around to manage communication in a respectful way. Only the person holding the talking stick is permitted to speak. Participants in the circle can elect to "pass"

3. There are some simple ground rules to protect the process

4. The teacher or student manager acts as a facilitator not as a controller of the process

5. A script is used to manage the dynamics and steer the process

6. The focus is on the incident and those affected, not what needs to be done to the wrongdoer.

Enhancing teaching and learning

These classroom conferences are designed to improve curriculum delivery, pedagogical processes and learner engagement. They can be used at the beginning of a new section of work, before a change in routine, at the beginning of each term or to evaluate a unit of work and its outcomes. They take nothing for granted and describe how things are to be in an explicit, relational framework. Of course school children will test these limits, but these disruptions will be managed in ways already understood by the students, because these processes have already been decided collaboratively. Ideally, these conferences will take place in a circle, with the teacher as facilitator. This meeting has ground rules, and follows a plan in the form of a script that assists everyone in the group to have meaningful input. Outcomes may be written down to be referred to later, or not, as the occasion demands. Some teachers will object to the "waste" of time this process takes. Others will see it as an investment that will save time in the long run. It is true that relationship development and maintenance takes time, but the long-term pay off is compliance, a sense of shared responsibility and improved classroom productivity.

The underlying theme and value in these kinds of conversations is that relationships matter.

Responding to wrongdoing

Whether you are faced with a small number of "wrongdoers", or a whole class which has been difficult in a chronic way for some weeks or even months, conferences designed to deal with wrongdoing, if facilitated carefully, can be extremely effective. Lectures, warnings, removal of students from class, detentions and phone calls to parents may be effective in the short term, but fail to address the emotional damage to the teacher or classmates.

---

† The circle is a very old, traditional approach to problem-solving in most cultures and remains intact in some indigenous communties
†† The talking stick is sometimes called a talking piece, and may, in some cultures, be a sacred object

In the long term, the issues will probably resurface, especially if the focus has been on an individual's behaviour that has been dealt with in isolation. The classroom is a community. A community is healthy when its connections between members are sound. It will function productively when all its members, including the teacher, feel safe and respected and as if they belong.

Wrongdoing disconnects and isolates people. So the solutions lie in finding ways to reconnect. This can only be achieved when people can face up to the damage they've caused, be accountable to the other members of the classroom community for this hurt, and are prepared to do whatever is required to make things right. And these outcomes can only be achieved in a climate where it's OK to talk about feelings, to be given opportunities to talk about what happened and how it came to be, and where there is a clear expectation from teachers and peers that the right thing to do is make amends. This will not happen in a punitive classroom. Teachers and students will take some time to get used to this approach. It may feel disconcerting at first – a

> *The classroom is a community.*
> *A community is healthy when its*
> *connections between members are sound.*

challenge for some, exciting for others. Once the class community gets used to this approach, there will be real opportunities to work together to address wrongdoing in constructive and meaningful ways. This approach is capacity building. In time, young people learn how to solve their own problems and conflicts, and can even influence how these things are done at home. These conferences, in circles, are scripted to assist the process move forward systematically towards repair. Ground rules apply. They will take longer than the preventative conferences, and this must be taken into account during planning. Careful preparation is vital. The process and script will vary slightly depending on whether there are identified wrongdoers or not.

Please refer to Chapters 3–6 for instructions about preparation and facilitation of these conferences. ■

Chapter 3

Working proactively – classroom conferences and teaching and learning

We must be prepared to articulate explicitly the boundaries of daily life in our classrooms, playgrounds and corridors – what is acceptable and what is not, what is important and what is not. But we assume too often that young people understand why a particular way of doing things is important, or the values that underpin our decisions and practices. If we adopt a relational perspective, as restorative justice suggests we do, then the quality of our conversations and group processes must reflect this emphasis.

If you have chosen a restorative, relational approach to the management of curriculum (what you teach) and pedagogy (how you will teach it), the questions to be asked to prevent wrongdoing and harmful behaviour might include:

- If I change the teaching and learning environment, how can I assist my students to adjust and respond appropriately?

- How will my students benefit if I provide explicit instructions about the behaviours required when I change the teaching and learning environment?

- What do I need to manage if I change the social groupings in my class?

- How can I develop whole of class protective behaviours to improve learning outcomes?

- How can I evaluate my teaching in a supportive way?

If the above questions are on your teaching agenda then proactive classroom conferences are an ideal process to provide explicit behavioural, relational and pedagogical statements. These would also explore the possible harms in classrooms that would be a result of inappropriate behaviours and should dictate the development of a range of explicit protective behaviours by the teacher and student.

The classroom conference provides a robust process to enhance teaching and learning outcomes while being explicit about limits and boundaries and emphasising the importance of relationships.

The conference is too useful a process to be used only for the resolution of wrongdoing. Classroom conferences establish a process that provides a link between curriculum and pedagogy and behaviour management.

This type of classroom conference can be used for:

- Introduction and implementation of curriculum topics and teaching strategies

- Negotiation and establishment of classroom rules and codes of conduct

- Peer tutoring and peer support

- Experiential and research based learning

- Assessment and reporting requirements

- Group work, cooperative learning and independent study

- Project and assignment work

- Student centred and group centred learning tasks

- Feedback about student or teacher performance

The following scenarios present some working examples of how the proactive classroom conference process can be adapted to the management of teaching and learning in classrooms.

1 Cooperative learning activities

Purpose

To introduce and organise cooperative learning as the chosen method of curriculum delivery. This conference process aims for several key outcomes:

- To provide a forum where all students participate collaboratively to negotiate classroom processes

- To provide explicit statements, given in behavioural and concrete terms, about curriculum objectives, assessment tasks and student behaviour expectations

- To reassure students about what is to be achieved and what it looks, feels and sounds like

Preparation

The classroom is set up with all students sitting in a circle with their teacher as facilitator. Time required will be about thirty minutes but it may take less time when you are more experienced. A talking stick is used to control communication. The following 'script' (in italics) is a suggestion only, but the general format is a useful guide.

Introduction

Thank you for participating in our classroom conference. This conference has been called so that we can organise our classroom for the next few weeks. The conference has some simple ground rules that will help us get through

this meeting with a minimum of fuss.

Ground rules

- One person speaks at a time. The speaker must be holding the talking stick

- No put downs or personal comments about others

- You have the right to pass

- If you are unable to follow these rules you will need to sit outside the circle, which means that you will not be able to have a say or have a vote

- Is that clear to everyone?

Our conference today will help us organise our next work topic on Mammals. At the start of the year we met and agreed to follow a set programme for the year. We now need to cover Mammals during the next three weeks. During this conference we will need to decide how we will organise this unit of work. It will involve us doing some cooperative learning by working in groups of five or six students.

Descriptive statement

When we participate in group work it means that we need to behave as a team. Your group will have people in it who are good at different things. Your group should be able to solve most problems and complete all of the set tasks because everybody can make a contribution. Your group will need to cooperate with each other and use everybody's skills and knowledge.

Questions to the class

- *Raise your hand if you have worked in groups before.*

- *When groups are working well what will it sound like?*

- *When groups are working well what will it look like?*

- *When groups are working well what will it feel like?*

- *What behaviours will we need from people in these groups?*

- *What jobs will I have as the teacher? What will the class expect from me?*

- *We have our classroom rules. What rules will we need to change for this to be successful and for all of us to have fun while we get the work done?*

- *Who will be affected if we cannot follow these rules?*

- *How will they feel?*

- *When groups are not working well what should we do? How should we respond?*

- *How will we know that things are going well?*

How can we choose our cooperative learning groups in a fair way?

Thank you for helping today. We have made some great decisions. We will have another conference in one week to see how things are going and how people are feeling.

As you can see, the script has endless possibilities. The intention of the conference is to state explicitly what the required behaviours look like, feel like and sound like, and to put fair rules in place through negotiation so that the activity will be given every chance to succeed.

2 Change of learning environment

Purpose

To manage the use of, and change to, a different learning environment including classes leaving the school for excursions, camps, industry visits, etc. Or it may involve the class using the school library, audio-visual room, gymnasium, computer laboratory etc. This conference process provides a forum whereby:

- All students participate collaboratively to negotiate classroom processes

- Curriculum objectives, assessment tasks and student behaviour expectations are made in explicit behavioural terms including 'not negotiable' rules

- Opportunities for clarification can be provided about what is to be achieved and what it will look, feel and sound like

Preparation

The classroom is set up with all students sitting in a circle with their teacher as facilitator. Time required will depend upon the complexity of the tasks and the demands of the new environment. Students on camp may meet in a circle each morning or a circle may be arranged when the class arrives at the library or computer laboratory. Other scenarios may see a quick conference called when students hop off the school bus after arriving at the sporting or educational venue. Students simply stand in a circle for a few minutes while the teacher takes them through some key questions. In these quick conferences with small groups a talking stick would not be required.

Introduction

Thank you for participating in our classroom conference. This conference has been called so that we can organise our visit to the library to work on our assignment. Let me

remind you about the ground rules for how we should behave during this conference.

Ground rules

- One person speaks at a time, the speaker must be holding the talking stick

- No put downs or personal comments about others

- You have the right to pass

- If you are unable to follow these rules you will need to leave the circle, which means that you will not be able to have a say or have a vote

- Is that clear to everyone?

Descriptive statement

Our conference today will help us understand what is expected of us when we work in the library. These expectations include how we are to behave going into the library, when we work in the library, how we leave the library, how we treat the books and other resources in the library, how we need to cooperate with others who want to use the same resource and how we relate to each other in the library.

Questions to the class

- *How should we go into the library?*

- *What about the noise level when we are in the library?*

- *When we say cooperate with others, what does this mean in the library?*

- *The library has a way to make sure that everybody can share the resources. Can somebody tell us how this is organised?*

- *What responsible behaviours would we see in the library?*

- *Who is affected when people do the wrong thing in the library. In what ways are they affected?*

- *How would they feel?*

■ *How should our class respond if someone does the wrong thing in the library?*

This script can be adapted easily for other environments. The key is to keep the questions in explicit behavioural terms so that students are clear about what is expected of them.

3 Feedback and evaluation

Purpose

To manage the evaluation and review of a unit of work and when the teacher wants to collect some informal feedback about the teaching and learning process.

Preparation

The classroom is set up with all students sitting in a circle with their teacher as facilitator. Time required will be about thirty minutes. A talking stick is used to control communication.

Introduction

Thank you for participating in our classroom conference. This conference has been called so that we can:

Evaluate the unit of work we have just completed

or

I can get some ideas about improving the way I taught the unit on mammals

or

Raise any issues or problems about how our class is going, or talk about the really good things happening in our class

or

Review the results that we achieved as a class on the mammals unit of work and see what we need to change for our next topic

This conference has some simple ground rules so that we can have this discussion with a minimum of fuss.

Ground rules

■ One person speaks at a time. The speaker must be holding the talking stick

■ No put downs or personal comments about others

■ You have the right to pass

■ If you are unable to follow these rules you will

need to sit outside the circle, which means that you will not be able to have a say or have a vote

■ Is that clear to everyone?

Descriptive statement

Our conference today will help us look at the work we have just finished on mammals. We want to talk about what things went well, what things we enjoyed, what things we need to change, what things I could do differently as your teacher and other questions you may want to ask.

Questions to the class

■ *How did you feel about the self-paced work booklets that we used?*

■ *What went well?*

■ *What topics were really enjoyable?*

■ *How did you cope with the homework?*

■ *What could we change for next time?*

■ *What could I have done differently as your teacher?*

These conferences give both students and teachers a great opportunity to review classroom programmes and improve the teaching and learning outcomes. They are very 'safe' ways for teachers to monitor their performance.

Restorative Practices in Classrooms

Note: Teachers should be aware that honesty on their part and the willingness to accept feedback is an essential component of a healthy and fair classroom. Some teachers are prepared to give students very critical, often hurtful feedback about their classroom performance and behaviour, yet are not prepared to make this a mutual process. This sends a message about double standards and a lack of integrity and often results in the erosion of trust. Teachers wanting to walk the restorative pathway need to understand that a fair classroom conference may involve students making comments ranging from 'it's boring', 'this subject sucks', 'what you did is unfair', 'you always yell at us'. Teachers may find some of this direct feedback very unsettling and/or hurtful at first. But if we are not prepared to change what we do as teachers, how fair is it to expect students to undergo change?

To ease your way into these feedback conferences you may wish to have a co-facilitator with you for the first few. It might be useful to have students write down their feedback ahead of the conference so that their issues might not be so surprising or confronting, and you can have recovered your composure sufficiently to discuss their concerns in a constructive manner. Restorative justice values concepts of collective responsibility and collective accountability. You must be prepared to walk your talk.

The empowerment and engagement of classroom conferences can transform uncooperative and unproductive classes into responsible, thriving environments with students who appreciate the collaborative environment, speak with mutual respect for each other, offer suggestions, solve problems, and feel connected because they are heard, understood and respected, and have a sense of belonging to the classroom community. ▨

Restorative Practices in Classrooms

Classroom conferences – responding to wrongdoing

The disruptive classroom

The disruptive classroom is an educational phenomenon that happens for a whole range of reasons: change of classrooms, turnover in staffing, relief teachers, change in curriculum and delivery, time of the day, a long school term, casual dress day, new students, students with particular needs that aren't being met. The list is endless. Whatever the contributing factors, the end result is loss of motivation, morale, harmony and productivity, and feelings of anxiety and resentment – for both teacher and students. In these classes, we find more "management" language than "curriculum" language being used – the teacher spends a greater percentage of class time trying to contain the disruption from a handful of students than teaching the lesson itself.

Some "out of control classes" may not, in reality, be as serious as is often reported in staff rooms over a restorative shot of caffeine. When the issues are explored in rational moments, it may only be about high noise levels and low-level refusal. What is of greater concern are those classes that are constantly disrupted by the surging undercurrents of chronic conflict. It has not been uncommon for students to report that the conflict has had a life of several years, ever since "X" happened. Clearly the matter had not been resolved in its early stages, and had gone on to skew dynamics in the classroom, playground, and possibly beyond the school gates.

We sometimes need reminding that classrooms are populated by children, adolescents and/or young adults undergoing enormous physical, hormonal, emotional and intellectual change. They come to school each day "trying on" different roles for size and trying to write their own life scripts. Awareness of "other" is not a strength at this point in their development – their brains are still developing. All of this will be happening right in front of our eyes in classrooms, whether we disapprove of the behaviour or not. An added complexity, of course, will be the competence and experience of the teacher in matters of curriculum, organisation and behaviour management. In a restorative setting, feedback to teachers and student administrators about performance or policy will be forthcoming and will be welcomed in a spirit of justice and fairness.

When we fail to respond effectively to classroom disruption, in serious cases it is not unusual to field parent requests to remove their child from the class, sometimes even the school. At best, a few lectures and warnings from student administrators may settle things for a while but the tensions build again and the problem behaviours persist. Or, in traditional fashion, we might remove wrongdoers, impose penalties or give warnings to them before returning them to class. Or, we insist on a whole-of-class detention in the hope that the deterrent effect of this intervention will "straighten them out".

Responding restoratively

Most, if not all, students, as well as the teacher in a class, are affected by the disruptive behaviour of a few. One benefit of the classroom conference process is that it involves the whole class rather than removing three or four of the wrongdoers who have been 'caught' to be sent to a student administrator. Removing students from the class for 'disciplining' often sets up another layer of unrest in the class ("What happened?", "Are you suspended?", "Did you tell about ...?") and further isolates the wrongdoers from their peer community. A restorative response has the added bonus of protecting the class and teacher from a possible 'backlash' if consequences for the wrongful behaviour are inappropriate. When classrooms become frenzied and emotions are running high we can sometimes make wrong (read unfair or inconsistent) decisions in efforts to regain a sense of control and order.

Incidents that involve chronically poor behaviour by most of the class will have caused dynamics all of their own. Things may have been so awful for so long that students cannot find words to describe what's been happening. Other classes may have normalised the behaviour and believe that this is what school life is like. The facilitator will therefore need to take care to focus sensitively on the emotions and feelings of students so that they are assisted to understand what is acceptable and what is not, both to themselves personally, and to the class or school.

> *What is lost in a punitive approach to classroom problem-solving is the opportunity to make young people accountable to each other...*

Making students accountable

What is lost in a punitive approach to classroom problem-solving is the opportunity to make young people accountable to each other, to develop their awareness about what ongoing harm is being done to individuals and relationships, to help them understand their obligations to their classroom community and have them participate in a democratic process to make things right. Real benefits of the restorative classroom conference include its potential to address the behaviour of all the students at the one time within the class and

> *Teachers must be prepared to model social and emotional competence and send a message that relationships matter.*

achieve the kind of outcomes described above. A punitive intervention could never hope to deliver such outcomes.

The classroom conference

Introducing the restorative classroom conference process is both challenging and exciting for students and teachers. Once incorporated into practice, teachers experience real opportunities to work with their students and address wrongdoing in meaningful and constructive ways. Students develop trust for the process, become less concerned about punishment and learn more effective ways to resolve conflict and repair harm instead of resorting to violence and disruption. After being involved in several conferences students realise from their experiences that:

- Classroom conferences offer a 'fair process'
- Retribution and retaliation from wrongdoers are very unlikely
- Wrongdoers show greater commitment to owning their behaviour when they understand that punishment is not on the agenda
- Teachers feel high levels of satisfaction and relief when they see their students as responsible people rather than dysfunctional 'monsters'
- Problems and issues do get sorted out because the school actually responds effectively and does something about what has happened
- Students demonstrate responsible and sensitive problem-solving skills when given an appropriate forum

Levels of student disclosure increase with each conference. Wrongdoers are less guarded in speaking about what they have done when they understand that conferences are not about punishment and stigmatisation. Wrongdoers are more likely to develop self-discipline and emotional intelligence when they are given opportunities to tell their story, be accountable and to then right their wrongs. Victims fearful and anxious of 'telling' or 'dobbing' on wrongdoers, when disclosing in safety have these emotions transformed to positive feelings of security, hope and power over future events.

Teacher involvement in these conferences is vital. While some teachers will initially be reluctant to share their real feelings about what has happened because of a fear of appearing vulnerable, they must be prepared to model social and emotional competence and send a message that relationships matter. They must be able to demonstrate that it is OK to talk about one's feelings. In our experience "heart-talk" from a teacher about their feelings of failure, embarrassment, frustration, worry and hurt has a far greater impact on young people than any abstract diatribes about the reputation of the school and rule-breaking.

The questions that need to be asked in the wake of a harmful incident might include:

- Who is responsible and accountable for what has happened?
- Who are the students and teachers in the class that have been affected?
- What might their needs be?
- What is the extent of the harm that has been done?
- How might we repair that harm?
- How can we get the wrongdoers to face up to what they have done?
- How can the class do that?
- How can the students and teachers prevent this happening again?
- What outcomes do I wish to achieve for my students, myself and other teachers?

Considerations for a classroom conference

A classroom conference should not be considered if the students deny their involvement in the incident. It is not necessary for students to admit or recount their every action or spoken word, just an admission that they did these wrongful things to people or property is sufficient. Restorative processes do not and should not resemble a court of law or any other adversarial process. Using a classroom conference to investigate who did what to whom and to apportion blame will do further harm.

When organising your classroom conference consider the following:

- How many students and teachers are involved?
- What is the student/s' history of wrongdoing?
- What are the risks of going ahead with a conference?
- How else are we going to make things better when all else has failed?
- What are the potential benefits for students, teachers and others?

All of these questions will lead to you deciding on whether an individual, small group, large group or whole class conference is appropriate to address the wrongdoing and repair the harm. The incident may only involve one or two students in your class, or the harm may have spilt over to affect other classes and other teachers. As classroom teachers you are the best people to determine who has been affected and what is the most appropriate conference format to implement.

In cases of serious wrongdoing that would normally attract a suspension or exclusion from school, you may well have to justify why it should be managed within your classroom with a conference. Perhaps you are a solitary 'pioneer' in your school wanting to incorporate restorative practices in your classes. This journey is not for the faint hearted and often leads to serious debate with others about long held values and beliefs concerning the school's responses to student behaviour. But the proof will be in the pudding, so do not be swayed by the pressure from sceptics.

We have designed the classroom conference to deal with two different types of situations. The first is designed to deal with blatant wrongdoing, where wrongdoers have been caught in the act, or have admitted their involvement, and all parties are willing for the incident to be resolved by a conference. The second deals with more amorphous/ambiguous situations where the dysfunction in the class has built over time, and any number of formal sanctions have brought no relief. No doubt there will be many situations you will find yourselves in that lie somewhere between these two. With experience you will be able to adapt either process to meet your needs. In some cases, parents will be informed either before and/or after the event, and will be made aware of any agreement reached.

Classroom conference – one or more wrongdoers

This conference is designed to address the harm caused by one or more wrongdoers whose behaviour has been seriously inappropriate and has affected a large number of classmates, but in your opinion, does not require participation of parents. This conference is convened only after careful preparation outlined below, and pretty much follows the conventional conference script.

Preparation

Preparation is critical for the success of this conference. The preparation may need to be done during class (students are organised to work on independent tasks while the teacher prepares) or in other 'free' time. It may also be appropriate to seek class release time depending on the seriousness of the incident. The following tasks need to have been done so that the intended outcomes are achieved:

- The classroom teacher has discussed with student administrators what outcomes they seek from the classroom conference

- Wrongdoers have admitted to their involvement in the incident

- Wrongdoers have agreed to have the incident/s managed by a classroom conference

- Victims have agreed to participate in the conference

- Teachers and student managers affected by the behaviour have been asked to participate and have some idea of the questions that will be asked

- The class of students as a whole are asked whether they agree to the conference

- Wrongdoers and victims have some idea of the

questions that will be asked by the facilitator

Before the conference begins the facilitator (teacher, student manager or administrator) must have a clear picture of the experience of victims, wrongdoers and bystanders. This will mean interviewing each key party separately. It is important to involve all students in the conference so that the wrongdoing can be rejected by the class, those most affected have input, both with their stories of how they have been affected and in the decision-making process, and sufficient support can be provided for the wrongdoers and victims. If someone other than the class teacher is facilitating the conference and they are unfamiliar with the relationships and dynamics of the class, it will be necessary to speak with others to find out who should participate as supporters for the victims and wrongdoers. It is appropriate to have these supporters sitting next to the victims and wrongdoers in the circle.

Briefing wrongdoers, victims and the class

Before the conference, you should meet with the wrongdoers separately so that they are given the choice of attending the conference and admitting to what they have done, or having their wrongdoing managed differently by the school (this may involve a meeting with parents, suspension etc). They must be briefed about what questions will be asked in the conference and about the opportunity they will be given to make amends. Wrongdoers must also be told that their classmates will be asked what needs to happen to repair the harm and that this will be recorded in a formal agreement. Some reassurance may need to be given about a natural fear of harsh requests for reparation from their classmates. Ask wrongdoers who they would like to have sitting next to them as a supporter, then let these supporters know what their role will involve. It is a good idea not to brief offending students as a group. This will avoid the risk of negative peer influence that may interfere with what you are trying to achieve.

Following this, a meeting is then organised with the primary victims (those directly affected), their supporters and remaining students. Without the wrongdoers present, brief the class about the stages of the conference: the telling of stories, exploring and repairing the harm, and making the agreement. Share with them the key questions that will be asked in relation to these stages. Inform the class as to where in the circle the wrongdoers will sit. Then, ask students where they would like to sit in the circle and with whom.

If you feel overwhelmed by the demands of what is involved in preparing a classroom conference then take some relief in the knowledge that less is required after classes have experienced a few of them. The scripted questions become familiar to everybody and the process requires less explanation. Indeed, students will become used to the format and philosophy as simply "the way problems are solved around here".

Facilitating the conference

It is important to follow the script and the order in which students are questioned. The reasons for this are explained in *Restorative Practices in Schools: Rethinking Behaviour Management.*

Introduction

Thank you for participating in this classroom conference. We have agreed that when people do the wrong thing and cause problems in our class we will meet like this and try to repair the harm. We are going to look at what happened on (date), when (names of wrongdoers) did (name the problem behaviour) to (name of victims). We want to find out who has been affected by what has happened and in what ways. We are not here to decide if (name of wrongdoers) are good or bad people. We want to find out what happened, what needs to be done to fix things, and what we can do to make sure that this does not happen again. You are all free to leave this conference at any time, but you need to know that the school will manage your behaviour differently if you do. Is that clear? Hopefully, we all sign an agreement at the end of this

conference and it will mean that we can put all this behind us.

Conference rules

We need to follow some rules so that everybody can be heard and treated with respect.

- One person speaks at a time. To speak you need to be holding the talking stick

- What is said stays in the room

- You may pass if you wish

- Tell us how you feel about what has happened, not what you think

- If you can't follow these rules you will be asked to sit outside the circle, which means you will not be able to speak or have a say in what should happen to fix things

To the wrongdoers: (to the most articulate and/or emotionally literate student first)

What happened, how did you get involved?

What were you thinking about when you did these things?

What have you thought about since?

Who has been affected by what you did?

In what ways?

To the victims: (the primary victim first)

What did you think when this happened?

How has this affected you?

What has been the worst thing for you?

To those who are closest to the victims:

What did you think when you heard about/saw what happened?

How do you feel about this?

What is the most important thing for you?

What concerns you the most?

To the rest of the class: (leave wrongdoer supporters until last)

What did you think when you heard/saw what happened?

How do you feel about what has happened?

What has happened since?

How has it affected you?

How are things now between you all?

To the wrongdoers: (address them all at once)

Is there anything you need to say to anybody here today?

Or

What do people need to hear from you at the moment?

Then, if necessary

What things are you apologising for?

To the victims:

What needs to happen to make things right?

What would you like to see happen to fix things?

To the class:

What else needs to be said or done to right the wrongs?

To the wrongdoers:

Do you agree to this?

Is this fair?

To the class: (victims, wrongdoers and others)

How can we make sure that this does not happen again?

What plans can we make?

What should we do if this happens again?

Closing the conference

I have written down what we have agreed that needs to be done by (names of the wrongdoers) to repair the harm. Who will take responsibility for managing this agreement? (a student is quite acceptable). Before finishing I would like everybody to sign the agreement and that will be the end of the matter. Is there anything anybody else needs to say? Thank you for participating in this classroom conference.

The no blame classroom conference

As an Assistant Principal, Dean or Head of House, your role may include responding to teacher's calls for support when classes become difficult, if not impossible, to manage because of those 'red cordial lunches and windy days' – where it is hard to put a finger on the cause(s). The 'no blame'[†] classroom conference is an adaptation of the conference process designed to resolve these very tricky and frustrating situations where no amount of consequences or sanctions will settle things. It is called a 'no blame' process because it does not seek to blame individual students for what has happened, but rather, to make the whole class accountable for making things right. In some cases it may be appropriate to follow up with a smaller conference to manage individual wrongdoers whose poor behaviour persists. This progression has been found to be successful in bringing about significant behavioural and relational changes in classrooms. It is an effective way for student administrators to get involved in classrooms and begin to work with students and teachers.

Student managers will find the 'no blame' classroom conference a valuable intervention to support 'emergency' or 'relief' teachers, inexperienced teachers and those having a minor crisis who call for help in their classrooms.

Preparation

You may be the classroom teacher and decide to facilitate a no blame conference for your own class when you sense that things are not right with relationships or that there is a degree of unrest and/or conflict. If you are a student manager called in to help, you will need to visit the class before the conference to ask students to prepare statements describing the 'harm done'. You may ask the classroom teacher to do this for you or you can ask for these statements immediately before students meet for the conference. If the latter is the case, it is best if students write these individual statements at their desks, before you set about organising the room for the conference. The class will only need to spend five minutes writing down what has been done to them or what negative things have been happening in the class. Students need to be reassured that this will be done confidentially, with all comments being anonymous. Try to have as many of the class teachers present at the conference itself as is reasonable. This may require relief arrangements to be made.

When asking students to prepare these pre-conference statements, say:

Thank you for agreeing to participate in a classroom conference which will happen shortly/tomorrow. Before we have our conference we need to understand what harm has been done to people in our class. I would like everybody to take five minutes and write down on the paper provided these things:

Write down what has been done to you – the verbal or physical harassment, the name calling or put downs etc

Write down what has been done to others in this class: the words or actions that have been used to hurt people, what you've seen and heard happen

We need to hear about the bitchiness, the pushing, the fighting, the teasing and rumours and the threats (whatever is appropriate)

*Please do not put any names on this paper. **Do not put your name or anyone else's on this.** It is confidential and what you write will not leave this room. If you need to write down something offensive that has been said, please do so. You will not be in trouble – we need to know exactly what has been happening.*

After the class have spent some time reflecting and writing, collect all the sheets of paper. After you have read the student's statements privately, choose those that will help give the class a picture of the harm that has been done. Be careful, when reading out these statements, that a victim is not identified

† Most of you will be aware that the term 'no blame' was first coined by Anatol Pikas in Sweden when he developed a less punitive approach for responding to less serious cases of bullying

by way of the names or labels used. The sheets will be rolled up after they are read out and secured into a baton. This becomes the 'talking stick'. Make sure you have tape or an elastic/rubber band handy. You are now ready to begin the no blame conference either immediately or in the next few days. Arrange the classroom chairs in a circle. It is a good idea to make sure that the class is not interrupted for the duration of the conference (at least fifty minutes to an hour), the public address system is turned down and you have a box of tissues with you, as there may well be tears shed.

Introduction

Thank you for participating in this conference. This classroom conference will take about one hour. This conference has been called because (please choose an appropriate statement or develop one of your own):

Your teachers can no longer successfully teach this class and many students in this class can no longer learn and people are being harmed by this behaviour

Or

Teachers and students have said that there are problems with people fighting and verbal harassment, which means that our class is not going well

Or

People have said that there is a lot of trouble and conflict in our class which is causing harm to people

Or

People are not being responsible for their behaviour and people's rights to learn and feel safe are not being respected

We are here to talk about the harm that has been done by the behaviour of this class. We want to try and understand who has been affected by your behaviour and in what ways. You will be given a chance to talk about what things need to happen to make things better. People in this class who have been harmed by the behaviour will be given the chance to talk about how they have been

affected. This is a 'no blame' conference. No one will get into trouble or be punished for what they say.

Conference rules

We need to follow some rules so that everybody can be heard and can make a contribution.

- What is said here today stays in this room
- One person speaks at a time. To speak you must be holding our talking stick
- You may pass if you wish
- Tell us how you feel about what has happened, not what you think
- If you can't follow these rules you will be asked to sit outside the circle, which means you will not be able to contribute or have a vote
- You may leave the conference any time you wish but you need to know that the school will manage your behaviour and what you may have done in a different way
- Do we need any other rules?

To all participants:

I will now read out some of the statements that you have all made. No names will be mentioned.

When the statements are read, roll them up and secure them to become the 'talking stick'.

I will now roll up all of these statements to make our talking stick. What should we call this stick?

To all teachers present:

I would like to ask the teachers present to tell us how they feel about what has been happening in this class.

How do you feel about the behaviour of this class?

What's it like to work with this class?

What are the main issues for you?

To the class:

We will now move around the circle and ask how people feel about what has been done to them and others in this class. Do not mention any names.

What has been happening to you?

How has this affected you?

What has changed for you?

What is the hardest thing?

How do you feel about what has been done to others?

How has the class changed?

What are the issues for you?

Use the above questions as prompts, especially with those students who are finding it difficult to speak.

After the circle has been completed once:

Raise your hand if the talking stick should go around the circle again.

Raise your hand if you feel that this harassment of people in our class and these problems need to stop. Thanks, hands down.

To the class:

We now want to explore who has been affected by the behaviour of the class. We will move around the circle and ask you to tell us who has been affected and in what ways.

As the talking stick makes its way around the circle, you may need to offer the following prompts:

Who else? Think of the people not here today.

Can anybody tell us how .... has been affected?

Raise your hand if you are surprised that so many people are affected.

Hands down, thanks.

To the class and teachers:

*Now it is time for some courage and honesty. We need you to take responsibility for what you have done. **Remember that what is said will stay in this room. No one will be punished.** Tell us what you have done and what you need to do to fix things. You do not need to mention people's names. You may want to say 'I have put people down by name-calling and to those people I apologise', or you may want to say 'I have pushed and punched Peter and Sam at the lockers and I apologise, I will not do this again'. Raise your hands if the talking stick should go around this way, or should it go that way? The talking stick will pass in this direction. Let us begin.*

As the talking stick makes its way around the circle, you may need to offer the following prompts:

What do the teachers need to hear from this class?

What things are you apologising for?

After the talking stick has circled once ask:

Does the talking stick need to go around our circle again?

What else needs to be done to make things better?

Do you accept the apologies that have been given?

What else would you like to see happen?

We now want to talk about what other people could have done to prevent the harm.

Who can tell us what other people could have done differently?

Who stood there and watched and listened and knew that it was wrong?

Who would do something about it next time?

Should the class take some responsibility for what has happened?

Making an agreement and planning for the future

What needs to be done to make sure that this does not happen again?

Do we need to make a formal agreement? Written down?

What should the agreement say?

Who should be responsible for monitoring the agreement?

What should we do if this happens again?

How can the class respond?

Who should decide what happens to the people who do the wrong thing?

Closing the conference

*Is there anything that anybody wants to say before we finish? Thank you for helping us with the conference today. **Remember that what has been said must stay in this room.** What needs to happen to this talking stick? Where should all of the harm and hurt contained in this stick be*

Individual, small and medium group conferences

We have adapted the conference script even further to manage the day-to-day, negative, inappropriate behaviour that students of all ages present on a daily basis. The wrongdoing in question is minor and would not warrant a classroom conference. These conferences are facilitated 'on the spot' and require no preparation. As you practise and apply these individual and small group techniques you will begin to understand the scope and flexibility that the process provides.

The following scenarios are designed to give you examples of how the conferencing script and process can be used to manage individual, small and medium-size conferences. They are not prescriptive, merely included to show you that you can adapt the process for any situation that is disciplinary in nature. These conferences are almost instantaneous and are facilitated anywhere around the school. There are only slight changes to the script and to the order of questioning. As you become more familiar with the language and script, so will your students. You may begin to hear students using the language amongst themselves. The teacher in these "on the spot" conferences may play multiple roles: facilitator one minute, victim or supporter the next.

Individual conference: a conversation with one student

The following two scenarios are examples of an individual conference being used as a brief intervention in the playground, classroom or corridor. There may have been simple breaches of rules: late to class, failure to bring class materials, refusing to share the tasks in group work, swearing, harassment and bullying at student lockers, exclusion of others. These individual conferences (a "restorative conversation") can replace those difficult teacher–student interactions that often encourage secondary behaviours because the teacher feels obliged to address the student's attitude. And this becomes a distraction that goes nowhere:

I wasn't hurting anyone, I gave it back, and anyway they did that to me last time! (hands on hips, one leg forward, head tilted to the side)

I finished my work and you said we can do what we like! (arms crossed on chest, challenging effect)

They always sit next to me. She smells and won't stop looking at my work! (loud, abusive and with a sneering face)

Scenario 1: Late to class

Sam is late to class, again. The teacher allows Sam to join the class with a calm "Sam, please sit down quickly and begin the work". When the class is on task or at the end of the lesson the teacher finds a quiet corner place in the classroom and conducts an individual conference with Sam. The teacher establishes equal terms with Sam, facing each other with heads at the same height (respect and dignity rather than superiority and humiliation before peers).

Sam, we need to talk about your being late to class

The structure of these questions is important, don't rush them. The question above is a statement about being late and there is no room for debate or denial. You have stated a fact. (Saying "Sam, we need to talk about your behaviour" or "Sam, why were you late?" will serve no purpose for either of you.)

Sam, what were you thinking/feeling about when you were coming to our class late?

This question asks for the background to the incident. You need to listen. This will tell you if Sam has poor organisational or decision-making abilities. Be prepared though, to hear "Your class is boring, I didn't want to come". Do not rise to the bait! Simply ask:

What have you thought about since getting to class?

This question may give you a picture of how Sam feels: whether he is remorseful, fearful of being punished, his place in the class, attachment to the school. Some students will be keen to make amends whilst others will be expecting the school to 'do it to them' once again.

When you come late to class who is affected by your behaviour and in what ways?

You may need to lead the student through this reflective question, but be careful not to moralise. Ask leading questions like "How about the group you are working with on the project?" or "What about me, what am I doing right now? What should I be doing? What about the rest of the class?" This is an opportunity for the student to learn about social responsibility. This question leaves the trivial, wrongful behaviour behind and investigates if the student is connected to the class, whether they have insight into their behaviour and if there is an opportunity to learn from this incident.

How has this affected you?

You may need to help Sam understand how his behaviour is impacting on his own learning as well as on his relationships with others.

What do you need to do to fix things?

Here is the agreement stage and the chance to make amends and to formulate plans for the future. Sam is asked to own his behaviour. You might make a comment here, which serves to reintegrate Sam. "Sam, you are a terrific student and I enjoy your participation in this class. Coming late is pretty silly stuff that is spoiling your good work".

What can I do to help you?

The teacher begins to share some accountability and offer support. Another glimpse into the world of the student may be available as the teacher 'patches' up the relationship with this important offer.

This most basic application of the conference script builds restorative language and proactive teacher behaviour into the classroom. The above dialogue should take only 1–2 minutes. How long does a detention or a notation in the teacher's book take? In contrast, what is the effect of a punitive approach on the student and on your relationship with them?

The process is applied with respect and dignity. The student is not berated or belittled in front of their peers. There is no power play, and the teacher and student explore the incident in a controlled, calm manner. The opening questions are non-judgmental and the student hopefully feels that the teacher is listening to them (one of the common student complaints about teachers is that they do not listen). The script blends nicely with other teacher micro skills as the responsibility for the behaviour is placed firmly with the student. The focus of the script is to engage the student in a conscience-building exercise so that they may begin to understand their own motivation and reflect on how their behaviour impacts on others.

Scenario 2: The 'artful dodger'

Tony always needs a keen eye kept on her. Her art classes provide the ideal unstructured setting for her antics to flourish. Whether it is annoying others or a complete disregard for the art room materials, there is always an issue that needs confronting. The teacher has spotted Tony stuffing a used paper towel behind a cupboard instead of putting it in the bin. Again, you will notice that the conversation will take only moments. The focus is on a remedy for the situation and does not concern itself with punishment. The relationship between teacher and Tony stays intact, and there is hope that future behaviour will be more thoughtful.

Teacher: *Tony, what were you thinking about when you stuffed your paper towel behind the cupboard?*

Tony: *Not much, didn't know where the rubbish bin was.*

Teacher: *What have you thought about since we have started talking?*

Tony: *I shouldn't have done it.*

Teacher: *Did you do the right thing or the wrong thing?*

Tony: *Wrong thing.*

Teacher: *Who has been affected by what you did?*

Tony: *You!*

Teacher: *How has it affected me?*

Tony: *You could be doing something else now.*

Teacher: *Who else? Think about the cleaners, or the next class.*

Tony: *Yeah, the cleaner will have to get it out, the other class will see it.*

Teacher: *What can you do to fix this up?*

Tony: *Put it in the bin ... I'm sorry.*

Teacher: *What else needs to happen?*

Tony: *I will clean up around the sink for our next class.*

Teacher: *A deal, thanks. Off you go.*

Small to medium-size conferences

Scenario 3: The missing wallet

Students are participating in group work, moving freely around the classroom. Towards the end of the lesson Ashley, in an agitated manner, informs the teacher that her wallet has been taken from her jacket, which was on the desk. The teacher was about to stop the class to conduct a search when she calls out that they have found her wallet on a chair. Then she calls out "Nicky took it". Nicky then calls out to the victim that it was "just a joke, I was only mucking around". The teacher quickly directs Ashley and Nicky to remain behind at the end of the class so that "we can get it sorted out". The teacher keeps an eye on both students until the end of the lesson. The class has left and the small conference begins. Try to imagine what each response would be as you read through the key questions.

To the wrongdoer and victim:

Nicky, Ashley, we need to sort out the incident with the wallet.

Teacher sits down with both students in a triangle.

Nicky, what were you thinking about when you took the wallet?

What have you thought about since it happened?

Who has been affected by what you did? In what ways have they been affected?

To the victim:

How did you feel when you noticed your wallet missing?

What was the worst thing about it?

To the wrongdoer:

What needs to be done/said to fix things?

To the victim:

Is there anything else that you would like to see happen?

To wrongdoer and victim:

Is this the end of the matter?

This is what we have sorted out today...

This small group conference should take only a few minutes. The punitive alternative to this could have been a heated argument with the wrongdoer who was 'playing a joke' yet behaved inappropriately. A lecture about personal property, theft and practical jokes may have had little impact on the wrongdoer, and the victim may have wanted to 'even the score' after class.

Scenario 4: 'Manners please'

This example is set in a classroom where students are working on a range of tasks including accessing the internet for a set period of time using a classroom computer. The class is working well as you move around the room. Two students approach you asking for your help to sort out a problem. Peter and Susan are not moving off the computer after their time has expired. You gather the four students and move to the corner of the classroom and hold a small group conference to sort out the incident.

Teacher: *Peter and Susan, what were you thinking about when you went over your computer time?*

Students: *We weren't going to move, they told us to 'get off'. If they haven't got any manners, why should we move?*

Teacher: *We will talk about their manners in a moment. When your time was up did you do the right thing or the wrong thing?*

Students: *The wrong thing.*

Teacher: *How are people affected when you go over time?*

Students: *Can't get their work done.*

Teacher: *Who else is affected by your behaviour?*

Students: *The class stopped working when they heard our argument.*

Teacher: *What were you thinking about when you told them to 'get off'?*

Students: *We were annoyed, they always hog the computer.*

Teacher: *Did you say the right thing or the wrong thing?*

Students: *The wrong thing.*

Teacher: *Who has been affected by what you said?*

Students: *Them, everybody in the class.*

Teacher: *What needs to be said to each other?*

Students: *Sorry for hogging the computer... sorry for being rude.*

Teacher: *What can I do to help?*

Students: *Can you move the clock to where the computer is. It's hard to see when our time is up.*

Scenario 5: Harassment at the lockers

This case study represents just one of the many incidents that teachers are asked to sort out by students. Those teachers who have positive relationships with students are usually the first port of call and requests are often made at the busiest time of the day and in the most inconvenient places – in the corridor, during playground duty, or on the way to an important meeting or a rushed photocopying job. How can we respond? Refer it to someone else who is responsible for student management and discipline? Or deal with it on the spot? This case study tells the story of how a teacher can manage the intervention for one of these complaints.

Three students approached a teacher on playground duty and reported that they had been harassed by three senior boys and they were sick of it. The teacher listened to their story to gain some understanding of what had happened. This was not the first time they had been tripped up and pushed into the lockers by the senior boys. The teacher offered the students a range of strategies to resolve the incident.

What would you like to see happen? Would you like the students suspended, some after school detentions, or the Principal to speak to them, or the Year Coordinator to manage this? Would you like their parents involved, or would you like to talk to them about this with me right now?

The boys chose to talk to the older students with the teacher. A messenger was sent to find the senior boys and ask that they report to the teacher on the sports oval. The teacher gathered the six students together and arranged them so that they were standing in a circle. The teacher introduced the reason for the conference:

Peter, Greg and Steven have made a complaint about being physically harassed by the three of you. They were given the following options to sort this out: to the Principal's office; calling your parents; sending you to the Year Coordinator; a suspension or some after school detentions; or to meet with all of you and talk about it. They chose to meet with you and talk about it. What do you think of them for making that choice?

The seniors commented that they must be OK for not wanting them to get into trouble. The teacher then asked the wrongdoers some key questions after hearing the basic facts from the victims.

To the victims:

Tell us what has been happening.

The boys said that they had been tripped up and pushed into the lockers every time the seniors came past them in the corridor. One of the senior boys did most of the pushing but the other two always joined in. A girl was hurt just the other day when she got in the way of the older boys.

To the wrongdoers:

Is this the truth? Is this what you did?

The senior boys nodded their heads.

The teacher continued by asking the ringleader and then his accomplices:

What were you thinking about when you did this?

Nothing. We were just having some fun and they didn't seem to mind. It's only now we see that they have a problem. This happens everyday at school and we're not the only ones. Anyway, they were mouthy and cheeky to us when they started at the school, and we just wanted to shut them up. They called me 'Stretch' because I'm tall and kept asking how was the weather up there.

The teacher said:

We will deal with their cheeky comments to you guys in a moment.

Have you senior guys been doing the right thing or the wrong thing?

The wrong thing. It was pretty stupid of us.

What have you thought about now?

I suppose now that we have been caught, we should not have done it. We didn't think it would be a big deal.

The teacher then asked:

Who has been affected by your behaviour, and in what ways?

Well, these guys and obviously the girl — we didn't know we hurt her.

Who else?

You? I suppose you could be doing different things than sorting this out.

Who else?

Us. We don't want to get a 'rep' as bullies.

To the victims:

How do you feel about what has been happening?

We felt too frightened to do anything about it. If we told someone it might make it worse. Really sad because Greg didn't want to come to school any more. Angry because they don't know how they hurt me when I hit the lockers. How can I fight back? These guys are huge.

What is the worst thing for you?

Not knowing when we will cop it again. Wondering if they will get us in the playground. What will happen if my mom finds out.

The teacher then asked the older boys:

Is there anything you want to say to these guys?

Yeah, we didn't mean to hurt you, especially the girl. Sorry for all the rough stuff.

To the victims:

What would you like to see happen to fix things up?

Well, we need to apologise for mouthing off. They probably would have left us alone if we didn't start. Sorry.

Do you guys accept each other's apologies?

Yeah, one of us should apologise to the girl. Let's shake hands.

The teacher then asked all the boys:

What can we do to make sure that this will not happen again?

We won't be cheeky again.

We won't push or trip you guys again. I suppose it's up to us to set a good example.

What can you all do to make our corridors safer?

Think about what we do a bit more. Have a word to people who bully others. Keep an eye out for pushing and physical stuff.

Is there anything else anybody wants to say? Can we put this behind us?

Just thanks for helping to sort it out.

If you had your stopwatch running you would notice that this intervention took no more than about five minutes. Can we afford *not* to invest this amount of time? Does the problem have to be escalated to someone further up the discipline ladder? It may be appropriate to inform the deputy or year level coordinator, so the incidents and their resolution can be noted somewhere in case the behaviour is a problem again, but consider how much time is saved if it is dealt with on the spot. Relationships are restored, the troublesome behaviour ceases, students feel safe again and the risk of retaliation is minimised. All without resorting to punishment. ■

Chapter 6

Facilitating conferences – understanding the script

Organising students and the room

If you are facilitating a conference for an 'experienced' class, which means they have already participated in a few conferences, it will be a simple matter of asking them to set up the room for a conference. If the class are novices at the process, it will need more structure and organisation on your part to move desks (out of the way) and chairs to form a circle. Tips include asking those students who you know will be easily distracted to sit with their backs to the windows or interesting display boards, making sure that the 'chair swingers' do not have desks or walls behind them to lean the backs of chairs against, asking the uncontrollable chatterers to sit away from each other, and spreading teachers around the circle so that they don't huddle together in one spot. Finally, make sure that the circle is uniform and that you can make eye contact with each participant. At this stage students may be restless and noisy. Don't try to control this. Just get on with the conference and the formality will quickly bring order. Get things into perspective. How long does it take adults to settle at the beginning of a staff meeting?!

Using the conference script

The script represents a plan, a 'mud map', to assist you in managing the conference process. As a beginner, you would be well served to stick closely to the questions and their particular sequence. As you grow more experienced, you may find it easier to adapt the script to a particular set of circumstances, but the fundamental purpose, the type of questions and the sequence ought to remain unchanged. Experience has shown us that getting the order of participant involvement right is one of the critical factors in determining positive outcomes. Playing with the sequence will make your job much harder, as you risk the process going awry. And for those of you familiar with the script used in the formal community conference, you will find few differences.

The introduction sets the scene and places you, the facilitator, in charge. It also, importantly, reminds students and teachers of the purpose of the conference, ie to acknowledge what harm has been done, to seek ways to repair that harm and make things right, and to minimise the chance of it happening again. It also reminds students and teachers that the conference's purpose is not to

Restorative Practices in Classrooms

judge anyone, but rather to talk about the impact of the behaviours on others. This is also worthwhile remembering when the dynamics of the conference become 'interesting' and the group moves away from this central task and philosophy. A timely reminder of the purpose is usually enough to refocus participants. As you facilitate the conference always have the conference script with you as part of the paperwork on your lap. Refer to it when you get stuck or need to include a quiet pause for participants to reflect on a significant moment.

Ground rules

These are explicit boundaries for acceptable behaviour and detail the consequences for unacceptable behaviours. It lets students know the "rules of engagement" for speaking – who, what and how. Depending on the location of the conference, the range of participants, and the wrongdoing involved, other rules may be necessary. After you have facilitated a few conferences, these rule adaptations will become second nature.

Be sensitive to cultural issues and practices. It may mean beginning the conference with a prayer, affirmation or a song. These beginnings (and endings) can be decided beforehand in discussions with the classroom teacher (if you are not that person) and student managers. As a rule of thumb, go with what allows students and teachers to feel appropriately respected, while you stay in charge.

Script

Introduction (to be used when there are identified wrongdoers):

*Thank you for participating in this classroom conference. We have agreed that when people do the wrong thing and offend others in our class we will meet like this and try to repair the harm. We are going to look at what happened on (date), when (**names of wrongdoers**) did (**name the problem behaviour**) to (**name of victims**). We want to find out who has been affected by what has happened and in what ways. We are not here to decide if (**name of wrongdoers**) are good or bad people. We want to find out what happened, what needs to be done to make things right, and what we can do to make sure that this does not happen again. You are all free to leave this conference at any time but you need to know that the school will manage your behaviour differently if you do. Is that clear? Hopefully, we can all sign an agreement at the end of this conference and it will mean that we can put all this behind us.*

Explanation

The introductions are usually performed in order around the circle. This allows you to describe the role of each student and teacher in this 'community' of people affected by the incident. eg "On my right is Peter, one of the boys involved in the assault. On his right is Michael, and next to him is Mrs Mackie, who is Dean of the year 7 student body and is here today to support Michael and Peter..."

Even though all of the students and teachers present may know each other, the introduction is an explicit statement of 'who did what to whom' and does not allow the wrongdoers, victims or supporters to deviate from their involvement, or responsibility. It also reduces pressure on the facilitator to draw out each story or admission from each participant.

Obviously, if the group is small and they know each other, it may not be necessary to do this step.

Script

For instance:

We will be focusing on a series of events since the beginning of term in which Michael, Jeremy, Bill and Jordan have been involved to some degree or other – the latest of which culminated in the assault which took place last Tuesday at the bus stop. We are not here to decide if any of these young people are good or bad. We are more interested in understanding what has happened, how it came to get so out of hand, what harm has been done, how we might repair that harm, and more importantly, how we might reach agreement to make sure this sort of thing doesn't happen again.

You are all free to leave this conference at any time but you need to know that the school will manage your behaviour differently if you do. Is that clear? Hopefully, when we all sign an agreement at the end of this conference it will mean that we can put all this behind us.

Explanation

If the conference is being convened to deal with a series of incidents over time, in which the 'wrongdoers' on one day are the 'victims' the next – eg chronic conflict – it might be beneficial to include all the young people's names in this introduction.

The meaning of 'differently' will vary with each circumstance. It may be that the incident will be handed over to the Dean or Year Level Manager, parents may then be involved or other consequences applied. Whatever the reason, it must be clarified with students before the conference, and at this point of the process on the day. As stories are told new wrongdoers may emerge, which is why all participants, not just the identified wrongdoers, are told that if they leave the conference the school will manage things differently.

Telling the story
(questioning the wrongdoer)

This first phase of the conference is vital and must not be rushed (a temptation for beginning facilitators). It begins the process of painting a picture of what happened and the circumstances that led to the incident. It is crucial that the questioning technique used does not deteriorate into the type of language and tone of voice used by school officials investigating an incident. Rather, be quietly persistent. It's important to everyone present that they understand all the parts of the whole story – wrongdoers' stories are as important as others.

Where there is confusion about the facts, seek clarification. Remember, the young people who have done the wrong thing have already admitted their part in it. This no longer has to be established. We are trying to understand their motivation and decision-making capacity. Victims need to understand why it has happened to them. We are also seeking to understand the life circumstances of the wrongdoer – these young people are often the most vulnerable despite outward appearances and attitude – so that, hopefully, appropriate support can be built into the final agreement.

Because your preparation has been so careful, and you know everyone's stories, you will have a sense of which extra questions you may need to ask of any participant at any stage in the conference. Often, important events have occurred amongst the group that need to be brought out at the conference. It is very acceptable to prompt participants so that these 'social markers' are heard, eg "Peter, when we talked about your involvement in this incident before the conference, you said that you told your mates that you didn't want to be involved. Can you tell us why you did that?"

If the wrongdoers are reluctant to tell their story (it may appear this way), it is worth remembering that a conference can be confronting and students will be nervous. Also, they may not be as articulate as we would wish and talking about what happened may be a real struggle.

Script

Wrongdoer/s:

..., to help us understand what harm has been done and who has been affected by this incident, could you start by telling us what happened?

..., when you pulled the chair out from underneath Matthew what were you thinking about?

..., and then what happened?

Or

Can we go back to the beginning again. There's a bit I don't quite understand. Talk about what was happening in the Technology class before you were asked to leave.

Or

How were you feeling when you came to school and realised that you would have to go to Grade Assembly and be with her again?

How did you come to be involved?

What were you thinking at the time?

Or

What made you decide to do that?

How did you come to decide to do that?

What was going on in your head at the time?

Explanation

Where there are multiple wrongdoers, you can decide whether to use all the following questions on each wrongdoer before moving on, or use one question and move through all wrongdoers one at a time.

Often it is useful to begin a question with a statement that allows for no ambiguity.

The direction "tell us what happened" may not be a one-off. You may need to ask the question many times until you are satisfied that the whole story has unfolded.

Responses to this will build our understanding of antecedents to the incident. Also, it will help us to understand the pressures in a young person's life and also the tensions within the class. It may be that a previous relationship existed where two parties were firm friends, and then something happened to sour the relationship. It sometimes happens that two families in the community have a history of conflict which is now impacting at school. Make sure though, when you ask this question, that you already know the answer (from pre-conference interviews).

These questions are critical to reaching an understanding of the motivation behind a particular act. It is tempting to ask "why did you do it?" in these circumstances because victims often have a strong need to know why it happened to them. When we ask "why" questions we begin to apportion blame. A more useful question is one that searches for antecedent circumstances and/or the young person's decision-making processes which may well have been flawed in our eyes, but which make perfect sense in his/her world. The class will have their answer to "why" when the young person responds to these questions.

Script

Explanation

It might be useful to ask, as well, "and how were you feeling at the time?" if they have not already shared that with you in answering the first question. Students and some teachers often give "feeling" answers to "thinking" questions; however, boys may need some help with this.

What have you thought about since the incident?

Or

What have you thought about since this has all happened?

What did you think when you heard about the incident?

You are likely to get a variety of answers here, depending on the capacity of the young person for self-reflection and their maturity. Some may already be remorseful about their actions. Others may be angry that they have got into trouble, or because they feel they have been treated unfairly. Others may not understand why there has been such a fuss. There are no right or wrong answers here – just a window for us to see into their thinking and emotional capacities.

Who do you think has been affected by your actions and in what ways?

This will give conference participants another insight into the emotional/social maturity of the wrongdoer, although those kinds of conclusions are more likely to be reached by adults in the group. Some young people will have very little understanding about the depth and breadth of the harm that has been done. They may well respond with answers such as "Mrs Mackie was really upset" or "He was probably angry with me". You will have to use your judgement at this point about whether or not to pursue the wrongdoer's understanding of the harm, or let the conference process do the job as planned. This is where the classroom conference is a powerful tool for conscience building and teaching emotional intelligence in a 'real' setting. With young people who have found it difficult to reflect on their actions, it is useful to move on and then revisit this question after hearing from the victims.

Exploring the harm

The purpose of this part of the conference is to uncover and expose the depth and breadth of the harm done. Students and teachers making up the classroom 'community' are now given the opportunity to share their feelings and thoughts about what has happened before, during and after the incident.

It is as if each participant has a piece of a giant jigsaw puzzle, and in laying his/her story out for the community to hear, a shared understanding about what harm has been done can be reached. This is a beginning, for some students, of lessons in empathy and self-reflection, concepts about what is right and wrong, and giving words and meaning to feelings and emotion. It may also be a key moment where students begin to take responsibility for their behaviour because the process is safe and fair.

The order in which students and teachers are invited to tell their stories is critical: victims first, then their student or teacher supporters, followed by the supporters of the wrongdoers. It is important that the supporters of the wrongdoer(s) hear others' stories before talking about their own experiences. If these supporters, regardless of whether they are teachers or students, are invited to speak before hearing these stories, they may defend and/or rationalise the behaviour of their friend before all the facts are known. Not following this 'order' risks upsetting victims and their supporters and this can derail the conference process.

With incidents involving no apparent victim (eg drug and alcohol incidents, truancy, destruction of flora and fauna) it is useful to start with people who became involved by following the chronology of events. Do not make up pseudo victims. Victims need to be real people, not administrative reputations or school images.

Script

Victims:

What did you think at the time?

What have you thought about since?

How has this incident affected you?

Explanation

An alternative question here might be "how has this changed the way you feel about being in this class?" or "how has this changed things between you and your friends?" Because you know something in particular which was gained from your interviews, you might ask a leading question such as "how has this affected things at recess and lunchtimes?", "what has been the personal cost to you?" Because these conferences involve young people, they may well not have the linguistic skills to describe their state adequately. From our experiences boys in particular will often respond to most "feeling" questions with "I felt sad or angry." Do not worry too much about this because they will be learning emotional literacy from the other participants as conferences become a regular process on the classroom calendar. Be prepared to change the language of the questions you ask to suit the maturity/age of the young person.

How did your friends and family react when they heard about the incident?

What has been the worst of it for you?

Or

What are the main issues here for you?

Sometimes when students and teachers are distressed, or very angry, a helpful question is:

If the person being questioned here is a teacher, the question might be adapted to "how did the other teachers in your staffroom react?". Where the victims include adults (teacher, school principal, canteen convenor, camp co-ordinator), it is vital that they be encouraged to share with others the emotional component of the harm, ie how they feel and the pressures/stress they may be suffering as a result. They may need to be coached before the conference to be willing to share this personal information. This personal sharing and vulnerability/humanity is more likely to have an impact on wrongdoers than any rational 'schoolspeak'.

Victim supporters:

What did you think when you heard about the incident?

How do you feel about what has happened?

What has happened since?

Or

What changes have you seen in your friends?

Or

What changes have you seen in your colleague?

As ....'s /friend/colleague, what has been the hardest for you?

What are the main issues here for you?

This group is likely to be upset about what has happened, possibly wanting revenge. To afford any relief to this group, it is vital that they be encouraged to talk about how they feel about what has happened. Teachers are particularly vulnerable to feeling helpless in the face of an injury to a child in their class, and this may often be masked by strong displays of anger. The questions opposite should allow the supporter group to express these strong feelings.

This section of the conference is one of the key moments when wrongdoers are most likely to recognise and then understand the impact of their behaviour on others and the harm that it has caused. If students are "connected" to their school, meaning they have a sense of belonging to people in their classroom community, then they are likely to take notice of significant others – peers and teachers.

Wrongdoer supporters:

It must be difficult for you to hear about the harm that has been caused.

What did you think when you heard?

How do you feel about what has happened?

What has happened since?

How has it affected you?

How are things in class now?

How are things now between you all?

Wrongdoer supporters will usually be classmates who may have been witnesses or bystanders to the incident(s). They may be defensive or angry about their friend's involvement. The first question is an acknowledgement of this. If they express surprise about the behaviour, explore why this is so. It will provide those present with a window into the young wrongdoer's whole persona, rather than just the "bit" that has caused the harm. If they are defensive, it may warrant asking "is what they did right or wrong?"

Restorative Practices in Classrooms

Acknowledging the harm and making apologies

This is the moment in the conference where the wrongdoer is given the space in which to demonstrate that they have understood, at least in part, who has been harmed by their actions and in what way. For the victims, it is most important to hear this acknowledged. Wait for the response. Use silence.

Owning their behaviour, acknowledging the harm ("I didn't realise"), and showing genuine remorse places them at the "mercy" of those present, and assists in the next stage of planning to make amends. Some young people who have poor social skills or lack any degree of emotional awareness and are therefore unable to "read the play", may have to be directed/assisted by you to make the appropriate response.

Victims have four primary questions that need to be answered through the course of the conference:

Why me?

Do you understand how you have hurt me?

Are you sorry for the things that you have done to me?

Will you do this to me again?

If the facilitator has followed the script closely and questioned the wrongdoer so that all participants understand the motivation and circumstances, victims will have had some answers.

Script

Wrongdoer/s:

Before we move on, is there anything you want to say to ... (the victim), or anyone else here?

If necessary:

Is there something ... (victim, teacher, etc), needs to hear from you right now?

Or

What things are you apologising for?

I get the feeling (name of victim) that you aren't satisfied that Max understands/is really sorry. What needs to happen to change that for you?

Explanation

If you sense that victims are not convinced of the wrongdoer's remorse through their apology or because their body language conveys a different message, it is beneficial to ask:

Agreement

This begins the stage of the conference where plans are made to repair the harm (making amends), put support structures in place for those in need, and re-think some of the classroom structures and practices that may have contributed to the circumstances. If there are issues that have not been fully aired, or needs that have not yet been met, it will become apparent in this phase. Most victims will be satisfied with acknowledgement and apology and less concerned with material reparation if you have facilitated the conference by following the script. However, if the wrongdoer has not owned their behaviour, acknowledged the harm done, or provided a clear understanding to participants of what took place, then victims and their supporters will make unreasonable demands. If you sense lingering resentment and anger you may have to re-visit the script.

Script

To the victim and their supporters:

What do you want to see happen as a result of this classroom conference today to make things right/repair the harm?

To the wrongdoer and their supporters:

Does that seem fair?

Is there something that you would like to see happen that might help?

To all conference participants:

Who will be responsible for supervising the terms of the agreement?

Let me just summarise what you have agreed upon.

Explanation

Allow plenty of time for discussion. As stated above, if this stage becomes heated, it will most likely be the case that people's needs have not yet been met. It might also be that a party's capacity to read genuine remorse on the part of the wrongdoer is impaired for some reason. A useful question to ask at this point might be "What needs to happen to convince you that she is genuinely sorry and that it will not happen again?"

It might be useful, too, to record in the agreement what will happen if the behaviour recurs, so that the wrongdoer is clear about future consequences.

It is important to ask the class for their ideas about how to make amends or what else the wrongdoers may need to do or say to right the wrongs.

If demands are made that are unreasonable or that wrongdoers object to, attempt to discover the need that underlies the request. Find out what outcome is sought by this demand, and then ask if there is an alternative, more acceptable way this could be achieved. A valuable outcome from classroom conferences is that students learn about fairness and forgiveness.

Make certain that items in the agreement are realistically achievable, and written in language which is concrete and easily understood, eg "Danny will help keep our garden weed-free and tidy in the last half of her lunch hour for the next three weeks. She will report to Mrs Deagon, who will be there helping other students".

The responsibility for monitoring the terms of the agreement will usually rest with a teacher, school administrator, counsellor or welfare staff at the conference. In some cases a student in the class is able to monitor the agreement when it involves easily managed tasks and will not put students at risk of harassment.

You read the list of actions and get final agreement to commit it to paper.

Restorative Practices in Classrooms

Closing the conference

Script

You say to the whole group:

I will now record the agreement that's been reached here. This will formally close the matter, subject to completion of the agreement. You will each be asked to sign it and it will be kept safe by ....

Is there anything else anyone wants to say?

Thank you all again for participating in this classroom conference. You have all worked hard to resolve this incident and the agreement you have reached should go a long way towards repairing the harm that has been done.

While I write down the agreement, which I will ask you all to sign before you leave, please enjoy the refreshments we have provided for you (if appropriate).

Explanation

Leave a little time for people to compose their thoughts, then say:

Having refreshments and time available at the end of the conference is a real luxury. A classroom conference will consume most of time available before a recess or lunch break leaving little time for 'breaking bread with the enemy'. But, if it can be arranged it is an important symbolic part of the conference ceremony. It is important that this part of the conference is not rushed, and that students and teachers have an excuse to mingle a little longer before they leave. This is the informal reintegration phase that should extend well beyond the conference proper. Place yourself so that you can observe the dynamics. If any one particular person appears isolated (they may feel too embarrassed to mingle) give some subtle cues to teachers or students to join them.

Facilitating the 'no blame' classroom conference

Script
Introduction

Thank you for participating in this conference. This classroom conference will take about one hour. This conference has been called because (please choose an appropriate statement or develop one of your own):

Your teachers can no longer successfully teach this class and many students in this class can no longer learn. People are being harmed by this behaviour.

Or

Teachers and students have said that there are problems with people fighting and verbal harassment, which means that our class is not going well.

Or

People have said that there is a lot of trouble and conflict in our class which is causing harm to people.

Or

People are not being responsible for their behaviour and people's rights to learn and feel safe are not being respected.

We are here to talk about the harm that has been done by the behaviour of this class. We want to try and understand who has been affected by your behaviour and in what ways. You will be given a chance to talk about what things need to happen to make things better. People in this class who have been harmed by the behaviour will be given the chance to talk about how they have been affected. This is a 'no blame' conference. No one will get into trouble or be punished for what they say.

Explanation

This introduction sets the scene and is often helpful in settling classes who may be returning from a morning or lunch break. It makes explicit the reasons for the conference and lets the class know what will be happening and what their roles will be. The conference rules ensure that participants feel safe and puts wrongdoers on notice that their behaviour will not go unnoticed and it is time to take some responsibility. Some of the rules may need to be adapted for student ages and classroom environments. Use your judgement for each conference.

Exploring the harm

I will now read out the statements that you have all made. No names will be mentioned.

We will move around the circle and ask everybody to tell us what has been done to them or what they have seen done to others. Do not mention any names.

Sometimes the harm caused has been so chronic, students are unable to speak of it, or have become inured and initially believe that there is no problem. In dysfunctional classrooms, students may not feel safe or able to communicate thoughts and feelings in front of their peers or teachers. If time or circumstance does not permit you to collect statements from students it is appropriate to say:

Script

I will now roll up all of these statements to make our talking stick. What should we call this stick?

To all teachers present:

I would like to ask the teachers present to tell us how they feel about what has been happening in their classes.

We will now move around the circle and ask how people feel about what has been done to them and others in this class. Do not mention any names.

Explanation

Students already have some ownership of the 'talking stick' since the paper it is composed of contains statements about their hurt and angst. Asking them to name the stick binds them further to the cause of addressing and resolving the harm done. Do not be surprised by the names offered by creative students. Ask for a range of suggestions and then take a vote. The talking stick will be very symbolic for some students. Wrongdoers might find it confronting to be in possession of the stick while victims may begin to weep (and some do) when taking hold of it. Be prepared for a range of responses.

Allow people as much time as needed to respond. Teachers are asked for their responses first. We want them to talk about how they feel about the wrongful behaviour and the harm caused. Reluctance to plan interesting lessons, sleepless nights, feelings of dread when coming to teach the class are some of the emotions and issues we want the 'elders' to disclose. You may need to respectfully prompt teachers to disclose how they feel rather than what they think.

'Teacherspeak' should be avoided as students will quickly lose interest when abstract and long-winded comments are made. Briefing teachers for just a few minutes about what you want them to talk about will help significantly in the exploration of the harm.

At this stage it is important to listen closely to responses as this will give participants some insight into what is right or wrong, acceptable and unacceptable, and what students (child, adolescent and young adult) may have thought was OK. Their answers will give some insight into the ability of students to reflect on how they have been treated and how they expect to be treated. Novice "conferencing" classes will respond very differently to those classes who are familiar with the process. Feeling safe and emotional literacy are key elements in building meaningful student contributions. Students will often talk about general details of incidents but find it difficult to relate what has happened to them personally. As facilitator you will need to constantly probe and redirect students to the task of providing the necessary understanding of the harm done.

Script

We have heard how this has affected your friends. Tell us how this has affected you.

Try not to speak for others. Tell us how you felt about this.

You have said that everybody does this at recess time, but what do you think about your behaviour?

Do you think that it is fooling around or having fun now?

Is all this mucking around right or wrong?

We have heard that teachers have been unable to teach the class and many students cannot learn. We have heard that many students have been harassed and bullied and hurt by people in this class. People have said that it was only 'mucking around' or 'just having fun'. Raise your hands if all this mucking around and having fun is wrong. Hands down thanks.

Explanation

Questions might include:

The facilitator can ask if the stick should go around the circle again if there is a sense that students at first have been reluctant to comment but after seeing the process may wish to take a turn. A key to the success of these conferences is the management of student disapproval of these behaviours by the facilitator. Be careful not to moralise or ask 'value loaded' questions. An example of this is when some students comment 'we were just fooling around and having fun!' Responses to these comments and motivations could include:

The intention is to help students become thoughtful about others and reflect on the impact of their behaviour. When good natured teasing turns into verbal harassment and physical play turns into bullying, we have a real opportunity to teach concepts of self-discipline and empathy for others. Often in these conferences students feel that the school is placing too many restrictions on their behaviour. They sometimes interpret these behavioural boundaries as all or nothing rather than degrees of social interaction. This is why 'zero tolerance' and 'no touch' behaviour management policies do not work. It is important that these moments are not lost so that we can teach social skills and set realistic limits.

This question requires proper framing to encapsulate the main problem behaviours. Things should not be rushed. This is a key stage of the process as it is when the class rejects the behaviour without denouncing the wrongdoers. Asking students to raise their hands if it is time that the harm/problems need to stop is inviting peers to reject the behaviour within a continuum of respect and support. Hopefully, this 'community message' will have more impact on wrongdoers than the usual range of options and sanctions practised by classroom teachers. Some students may not have considered that the behaviour being discussed is harmful. The conference process aims to reject these behaviours so that students, and in some cases teachers, do not normalise these actions. Wrongdoers are hopefully given a clear message by their peers that the behaviour is wrong and unacceptable but they still have a place in the classroom community.

Script

To all participants:

We now need to explore who has been affected by the behaviour of the class and in what way.

Raise your hands if you are surprised by the number of people affected by what has happened.

Thanks, hands down.

Acknowledging the harm, taking responsibility and apologies

To all class members:

Now it is time for some courage and honesty. We need you to take responsibility for what you have done. **Remember that what is said will stay in this room. No one will be punished.** *Tell us what you have done and what you need to do to fix things. You do not need to mention people's names.*

Explanation

At this point the conference process aims to help the class understand that the whole school community is usually affected in some way: parents, student administrators, many teachers, others classes, the students themselves, the school principal etc. Give examples of how people have been affected – eg 'We've just heard that some of you don't want to come to school because of this class' – so that the conference is a learning experience and encourages students to be thoughtful about their behaviour. If there aren't many others affected beyond the class, spend time exploring in some depth how these few have been impacted. Here is another chance to build some empathy and promote social responsibility.

This is a key moment in the conference. First, ask the group which way the talking piece should travel around the circle. The talking piece may need to go around several times as students realise that it is safe to admit to what they have done and that they will not be punished or labelled. This process may begin slowly with many students passing, but it will pick up speed as students take cues from their peers. If admissions and apologies do not begin it is appropriate to give some prompts and examples: "I have called people names and pushed people at the lockers. I am sorry and I will try not to do this again", "I have stopped the class from working and I have put people down and I am sorry, I will not do this again".

It is at this point that students are compelled to 'own their behaviour'. A further outcome is that students learn that it is safe to take responsibility for their behaviour because the environment is non-punitive. As students acknowledge the harm caused and make amends they are 'reintegrated' back into the class. And the toxic, negative feelings that teachers and students may be experience can be 'transformed' into positive feelings of forgiveness, hope and optimism.

Script

Agreement

To the victims:

What else needs to be done to make things better?

Do you accept the apologies that have been given?

What else would you like to see happen?

Is there something that we have not understood?

Has something happened that we don't know about?

Has someone not taken responsibility for what they have done?

We now want to talk about what other people could have done to prevent the harm.

To all participants:

What needs to be done to make sure that this does not happen again?

How should we deal with problems and the resulting harm in our class in the future?

Explanation

The class and teachers are invited to say what else needs to happen to repair the harm. When wrongdoers have not taken responsibility for what they did or when victims are unable to pick up a display of remorse some tension may be present. This will be seen by people asking for inappropriate penalties and claiming that someone didn't 'own up'. At this point it is appropriate to ask:

Here the conference aims to teach pro-social skills and build in some protective behaviours for the future. It is important for students to understand what mutual obligation and collective accountability involves. Research tells us that involving peer observers and supporters is an effective way to reduce bullying and harassment. 'Dobbing in' and 'telling on' others can be reframed as a preventative strategy (getting help and supporting each other) and a cultural change occurs as students see that they are not putting friends in a position where they could be punished.

Some direction may be given to 'teach' the class about wrongdoing and mistakes. Students need to understand that making mistakes are a normal part of human behaviour, but it is how we address these wrongdoings that is important.

Often young people feel that reporting an incident is a waste of time as 'nothing happens' or 'teachers don't do anything'. Students need to be encouraged to contribute to an agreement so that plans are put in place which they feel will safeguard their class. Wrongdoers will also be clear about how the class will address future wrongdoing by them and by others. The conference process encourages positive behaviour by handing over responsibility for future consequences to the class and promoting protective behaviours. ■

Restorative Practices in Classrooms

What if?

I have facilitated a lot of individual and small group conferences with a wrongdoer but he/she keeps doing the wrong thing in my class or around the school!

It is not unusual for some young people to have periods of chronic low-level problem behaviour – 'stuck in a rut' with time being the only cure. Others may be trying out different roles and experimenting with their individual life scripts. Be clear and specific about the repeated wrongful behaviour. Is it the same behaviour repeated or different behaviours being played out? Your conferencing is having some impact if the original identified behaviour does not occur again. If you are conferencing the same behaviour time after time then the process is clearly not having an impact. It is also important to remember that while conferencing may be therapeutic, it is no substitute for therapy.

Think about moving to a larger group or whole class conference format where significant others (peers) can reject the behaviour and help to further explore the harm whilst still supporting the wrongdoer. Your final option of course will be to involve parents in a full community conference.

Doesn't putting the bullies and victims in the same room re-victimise the victim and empower the wrongdoers?

Current research tells us that punishment is not effective in changing bullying behaviour. In fact it places victims further at risk for 'dobbing'. Sometimes our responses impose harsh penalties on the bullies thinking that this is what the victim would want, not realising that we may have made things worse. Victims mostly want to be left alone, to feel safe and perhaps find out "why me?" The victims of bullying may also be fearful that if they speak up in a conference they will invite retaliation from the wrongdoers, or, if they speak about how bad it has been for them, that the bullies will 'get off' on this information, and their behaviour will intensify.

At the time of writing this manual it is evident to us that a restorative approach is the best answer. Re-victimisation is minimised when victims are provided with support from significant others, given choices about outcomes, and have their needs met by being believed and validated. Wrongdoers are provided with the same choices and opportunities in a process free from punishment. Research also tells us that bystanders and supporters need to be included in meaningful dialogue so that everybody can learn to take some responsibility for bullying in their school. classroom conferences are an ideal way to deal with bullying behaviour so that students themselves remove bullying from the agenda. From our experience, bullies can show true remorse, take responsibility for what they have done, and learn about the harm that they have caused in the conference process.

And as part of any classroom agreement, it might be suggested that if the behaviours persist, another conference will be convened – this time with parents involved.

What if I only get half way through the conference and the class has to leave?

As your experience grows so will your judgement about how much time is needed for each conference format. As a rule of thumb, a classroom conference with three or four wrongdoers and about twenty five students will take at least one full hour – and only when the class is experienced in the process. It may be impossible to have this time available, so split the conference up into sections and explain this to the class. For serious incidents that must be resolved before the class comes back together for lessons, it will be necessary to arrange release for the facilitator, dedicate a room for the conference and cancel the class programme for the morning or afternoon. You cannot afford to leave a class to go about their daily business with resentment, anger, distress, fear and retribution swirling around in students' minds.

In general, don't stop a conference midway through an important phase. There could be significant stories, reactions and feelings that might be lost. Inform the class that the conference will be continued as soon as can be arranged and tell them to be careful with each other until then.

We have planned a conference but parents do not want their child to participate.

It is not usual for parents to be contacted about individual, small group, large group or whole class conferences. In 'restorative' schools they are seen as part of the normal school day and one of the 'tools' used in student management. Included in the appendix is a letter that may be used to inform parents about a classroom conference conducted to manage wrongdoing where their child was one of the wrongdoers – after the event. It will be a decision for your school to make in line with other policies around informing parents of any concerns about behaviour. If, however, parents find out ahead of time, you will need to be prepared to inform them of your plans and motives.

It may not be appropriate for parents to participate in, or observe, a classroom conference without all other parents having been contacted, informed, and then invited to attend the conference. You can imagine the result of this process! So you will need to manage each case at it arises. If it is the parent of a wrongdoer, take time to explain the consequences if the child does not participate. Take care to paint a picture of how fair and respectful the process is. Inform the parent that their child has taken some responsibility for their actions because they have chosen to attend the conference. Then ask the parent what they would like to see happen. If they refuse to allow their child to participate inform them that things will need to be managed differently by the school. All is not lost as the next best alternative is a smaller conference with the wrongdoer and parents and hopefully the victim and parents. Parents of victims will often have reservations about their children participating. They may want stronger action or have concerns about further harm. You will need to pitch your conversation towards the benefits for victims and provide a clear picture of what the conference will look like.

Parents may find out about the conference from their children over the evening meal or even from a mobile phone message. If you have done your job in preparing the conference, many students will be relieved and even excited to tell their parents about the impending event. If students are fearful or anxious about the conference, parents might pick up on this and will be in contact with you. Explore their anxieties with them and reassure them about the philosophy, process and hoped-for outcomes. Let them know you will report back quickly. Some schools explain and advertise conferencing to their communities through pamphlets, newsletters and information evenings.

What if the family want the incident to be formally handled by the principal, police or civil action?

Serious incidents would normally be managed by a community conference which is beyond the scope of this manual. But, if a classroom conference is planned, it will be important to provide sufficient detail to parents about the whole process and to assure them that it will not exclude other sanctions or actions if they are not satisfied with the outcomes from the conference. From our experience, the need for further action is extremely rare. Again, if parents' concerns are so great, it would be best to consider a full community conference so that they may be included in the process of resolution.

What if a student discloses information about a crime or details of unknown sexual or physical abuse? Should the conference stop immediately?

Common sense is the best tool here. The conference process provides the safety and security for students to sometimes voice very secret and personal things. Your next move will depend on the circumstances and ages of those involved. You may be mandated to report these disclosures to relevant authorities. If the perpetrator is present as a participant, depending on their age, a complete end to the conference may be the best course of action. On the other hand if the focus of the conference is not diverted by this revelation, you may continue. As facilitator, acknowledge what has been said and provide an opportunity to address this after the conference.

What if the facts about the incident don't match and individual stories are confusing?

You must be as certain as possible of the circumstances before facilitating the conference. If the admissions by the wrongdoers and the stories of the victims are inconsistent and muddy, then more work needs to be done by speaking to others who may be able to shed some light on what happened. The main issue here is that the confusion of stories will become evident in the conference and time will be wasted trying to establish the facts, with possible accusations about lying and victims showing anger or reluctance to help clarify who, what and when facts. Exact details do not need to match, but who did what to whom and when, needs to be understood. If the class generally agree that harm was done, and that harm can be explored and talked about, that may be sufficient.

What if there is a concern that these wrongdoers will give each other support in the conference and treat it as a joke?

This is a common concern! Negative and unhelpful 'peer support' between a small group of students can upset your conference. To counter this undesirable behaviour, you will need to get things right from the beginning. Your pre-conference interviews should be conducted on an individual basis. This will begin to formalise the process of taking responsibility for actions and behaviours. Make it clear that attendance is optional and what the consequences will be if they choose not to attend, or decide to leave during the conference, or decide not to follow the agreement. Arrange your seating plan to have a supporter between each wrongdoer so that there is some separation. You need a card up your sleeve during the conference if wrongdoers begin to deny their involvement or denigrate the process. Use your judgement if you need to stop the conference and say: "You have chosen to attend this conference and take responsibility for what you have done, including acknowledging the harm you have caused. Are you now deciding not to do that?" If they agree that they no longer wish to be accountable for what they have done the conference must stop or be continued with only those wrongdoers prepared to participate openly. This will only be an issue in rare cases and the risk is greatly minimised by careful preparation.

What if the wrongdoer/s show apparent contempt by smiling or laughing, or inappropriate body language?

Often this behaviour demonstrates embarrassment, shame, fear or a lack of social skills, particularly with understanding social cues. This seemingly inappropriate behaviour may be an issue especially when apologies are made. Students will be quick to comment that "They don't mean it", or "It's easy to say". In this case ask the wrongdoer "What things are you apologising for?" or "You are telling us that you are sorry. Do you think you are showing us that at the moment?"

What if the class and victim/s make unreasonable demands to repair the harm?

These unreasonable demands often highlight several 'process' issues with a conference. As facilitator your task is to move the conference to the point where wrongdoers have owned their behaviour and understood the harm done by their actions. If this hasn't happened it can be explained by:

- The wrongdoer/s have not told enough of their story for participants to feel that they have taken responsibility for what happened

- The wrongdoer/s are not showing signs of genuine remorse

- The harm done has not been explored sufficiently for the wrongdoer to understand the impact of their behaviour

- There are other things that have happened that were not detected or heard during the planning stages and they remain unspoken

- The right people are not participating in the conference

- The facilitator is showing bias or is trying to counsel individuals

You might overcome this obstacle by handing the problem over to the class and saying: "We seem to be stuck here. Is there something we haven't heard or something that we don't understand? What is unfair here? What else needs to happen?"

In your pre-conference planning with victims you may need to give some guidance when discussing what things would make a fair outcome from the conference. In cases of chronic conflict that may have their origins going back years, it is worth the time spent exploring these histories. If not, they may become impediments to any healing and restoration that is attempted in conferences.

Should I conduct the conference if one of the wrongdoers is away on the day?

In schools and classrooms where conferencing is new, it would not be uncommon for wrongdoers and victims to avoid attending the day of the conference. With time, experience and good planning these fears will diminish and students will eagerly attend regardless of their role or involvement. In odd cases where students stay away, you will need to decide whether the school should manage their behaviour differently, whether the conference goes ahead or is cancelled until all can be present or whether another conference is organised. To help with your decision about whether to go ahead or not, consider whether you will achieve the desired outcomes if certain players are absent and whether fair processes be provided for all students.

What if the wrongdoer/s refuse to abide by the agreement?

It is rare that compliance with the agreement is a problem. Younger students will need help and guidance to complete some tasks and often it is their organisational skills that let them down. If the wrongdoer/s fail to meet their obligations, convene a small meeting with key people to explore the obstacles to compliance. Every effort should be made to assist young people to meet their obligations. If the incident involves harassment or bullying, then part of the agreement should state what will happen if the behaviour occurs again. This will go a long way to making the victim/s begin to feel safe.

During a conference I asked a participant to leave the circle because of their behaviour. They now want to participate and have promised to behave. Other students want them to join in as well.
What should I do?

Ground rules are ground rules! If this is the first conference for the class it will serve as a meaningful lesson in what is acceptable and what is not. The student should not rejoin the conference! If other students pressure you to let them back into the circle politely ask them to leave the circle as well. Students will soon realise that individual accountability is more important than groups and cliques operating in a conference. Please do not fall into the trap of having a show of hands if student 'X' can rejoin the conference. This will set up an immediate power play and do harm to those lower on the 'social ladder'. It will also dent your credibility as facilitator. ∎

Classroom conference script

Introduction

*Thank you for participating in this classroom conference. We have agreed that when people do the wrong thing and cause problems in our class we will meet like this and try to repair the harm. We are going to look at what happened on (**date**), when (**names of wrongdoers**) did (**name the problem behaviour**) to (**name of victims**). We want to find out who has been affected by what has happened and in what ways. We are not here to decide if (**name of wrongdoers**) are good or bad people. We want to find out what happened, what needs to be done to fix things, and what we can do to make sure that this does not happen again. You are all free to leave this conference at any time, but you need to know that the school will manage your behaviour differently if you do. Is that clear? Hopefully, we will all sign an agreement at the end of this conference and it will mean that we can put all this behind us.*

Conference rules

We need to follow some rules so that everybody can be heard and treated with respect.

- One person speaks at a time. To speak you need to be holding the talking stick
- What is said stays in the room
- You may pass if you wish
- Tell us how you feel about what has happened, not what you think
- If you can't follow these rules you will be asked to sit outside the circle, which means you will not be able to speak or have a say in what should happen to fix things.

To the wrongdoers:

What happened and how did you get involved?

What were you thinking about when you did these things?

What have you thought about since?

Who has been affected by what you did?

In what ways?

To the victims:

What did you think when this happened?

How has this affected you?

What has been the worst thing for you?

Victim supporters:

What did you think when you heard about/saw what happened?

How do you feel about this?

What is the most important thing for you?

What concerns you the most?

To the rest of the class (leave wrongdoer supporters until last):

What did you think when you heard/saw what happened?

How do you feel about what has happened?

What has happened since?

How has it affected you?

How are things now between you all?

To the wrongdoers:

Is there anything you need to say to anybody here today?

Or

What do people need to hear from you at the moment?

Then, if necessary

What things are you apologising for?

To the victims:

What needs to happen to make things right?

What would you like to see happen to fix things?

To the class:

What else needs to be said or done to right the wrongs?

To the wrongdoers:

Do you agree to this?

Is this fair?

To the class (victims, wrongdoers and others):

How can we make sure that this does not happen again?

What plans can we make?

What should we do if this happens again?

Closing the conference

*I have written down what we have agreed that needs to be done by (**names of the wrongdoers**) to repair the harm. Who will take responsibility for managing this agreement?(**a student is quite acceptable**). Before finishing I would like everybody to sign the agreement and that will be the end of the matter. Is there anything anybody else needs to say? Thank you for participating in this classroom conference.*

The 'no blame' conference script

Introduction to class

Thank you for agreeing to participate in a classroom conference which will happen shortly/tomorrow. Before we have our conference we need to understand what harm has been done to people in our class. I would like everybody to take five minutes and write down on the paper provided these things:

Write down what has been done to you – the verbal or physical harassment, the name calling or putdowns etc

Write down what has been done to others in this class – the words or actions that have been used to hurt people – what you've seen and heard happen

We need to hear about the bitchiness, the pushing, the fighting, the teasing and rumours and the threats (whatever is appropriate)

Please do not put any names on this paper. **Do not put your name or anyone else's on this.** *It is confidential and what you write will not leave this room. If you need to write down something offensive that has been said, please do so. You will not be in trouble – we need to know exactly what has been happening.*

Introduction to the conference

Thank you for participating in this conference. This classroom conference will take about one hour. This conference has been called because (please choose an appropriate statement or develop one of your own):

Your teachers can no longer successfully teach this class and many students in this class can no longer learn and people are being harmed by this behaviour.

Or

Teachers and students have said that there are problems with people fighting and verbal harassment, which means that our class is not going well.

Or

People have said that there is a lot of trouble and conflict in our class which is causing harm to people.

Or

People are not being responsible for their behaviour and people's rights to learn and feel safe are not being respected.

We are here to talk about the harm that has been done by the behaviour of this class. We want to try and understand who has been affected by your behaviour and in what ways. You will be given a chance to talk about what things need to happen to make things better. People in this class who have been harmed by the behaviour will be given the chance to talk about how they have been affected. This is a 'no blame' conference. No one will get into trouble or be punished for what they say.

Conference rules

We need to follow some rules so that everybody can be

heard and can make a contribution.

- *What is said here today stays in this room*

- *One person speaks at a time. To speak you must be holding our talking stick*

- *You may pass if you wish*

- *Tell us how you feel about what has happened, not what you think*

- *If you can't follow these rules you will be asked to sit outside the circle, which means you will not be able to contribute or have a vote*

- *You may leave the conference any time you wish, but you need to know that the school will manage your behaviour and what you may have done in a different way*

- *Do we need any other rules?*

To all participants:

I will now read out some of the statements that you have all made. No names will be mentioned.

I will now roll up all of these statements to make our talking stick. What should we call this stick?

To all teachers present:

I would like to ask the teachers present to tell us how they feel about what has been happening in this class.

How do you feel about the behaviour of this class?

· ·

What's it like to work with this class?

What are the main issues for you?

To the class:

We will now move around the circle and ask how people feel about what has been done to them and others in this class. Do not mention any names.

What has been happening to you?

How has this affected you?

What has changed for you?

What is the hardest thing?

How do you feel about what has been done to others?

How has the class changed?

What are the issues for you?

After the circle has been completed once:

Raise your hand if the talking stick should go around the circle again.

Raise your hand if you feel that this harassment of people in our class and these problems need to stop. Thanks, hands down.

To the class:

We now want to explore who has been affected by the behaviour of the class. We will move around the circle and ask you to tell us who has been affected and in what ways.

Who else? Think of the people not here today.

Can anybody tell us how .... has been affected?

Raise your hand if you are surprised that so many people are affected.

Hands down, thanks.

To the class and teachers:

*Now it is time for some courage and honesty. We need you to take responsibility for what you have done. **Remember that what is said will stay in this room. No one will be punished.** Tell us what you have done and what you need to do to fix things. You do not need to mention people's names. You may want to say 'I have put people down by name-calling and to those people I apologise', or you may want to say 'I have pushed and punched Peter and Sam at the lockers and I apologise, I will not do this again'. Raise your hands if the talking stick should go around this way, or should it go that way? The talking stick will pass in this direction. Let us begin.*

What do some teachers and students need to hear from this class?

What things are you apologising for?

Do people need to hear anything from you?

After the talking stick has circled once ask:

Does the talking stick need to go around our circle again?

What else needs to be done to make things better?

Do you accept the apologies that have been given?

What else would you like to see happen?

We now want to talk about what other people could have done to prevent the harm.

Who can tell us what other people could have done differently?

Who stood there and watched and listened and knew that it was wrong?

Who would do something about it next time?

How can the class take some responsibility for what has happened?

Making the agreement

What needs to be done to make sure that this does not happen again?

Do we need to make a formal agreement? Written down?

What should the agreement say?

Who should be responsible for monitoring the agreement?

What should we do if this happens again?

How can the class respond?

Who should decide what happens when people do the wrong thing?

Closing

*Is there anything that anybody wants to say before we finish? Thank you for helping us with the conference today. **Remember that what has been said must stay in this room.** What needs to happen to this talking stick? Where should all of the harm and hurt contained in this stick be placed? Does anybody have any suggestions?*

Please help us to fix up the classroom before we leave.

Classroom conference report

Date [   ]   **Class** [   ]

Teacher [   ]   **Facilitator** [   ]

Background to the conference

Identified wrongdoers/Problem behaviours

Agreement reached

Agreement will be monitored by

....

Classroom conference evaluation

Please complete this evaluation about the conference in which you have just participated. It will give us some feedback about the process and show us how we might improve it.

1.   Please circle your role in the conference:

Student   Teacher   Student Manager

Supporter   Observer   Other

2.   In general, what was the conference like for you? (please circle or add comments)

Excellent   Very good   OK   Not so good   Awful

3.   Was the conference a fair way to resolve what happened?

Yes   No   Other:

4.   Do you feel the same about things after the conference as you did before?

5.   Were you able to say how you felt or what you thought about what happened?

6.   Did it help you to hear other people's stories? How?

7.   Was the agreement at the end of the conference fair? Explain your answer.

8.   Do you think things will be different after this conference? If not, why not?

9.   Is there anything else you would like to say about the conference?

Conference facilitator checklist

Responding to harm and wrongdoing

☐ Find out all the facts from key students and teachers

☐ Meet with student managers to discuss the outcomes sought from the conference

☐ Meet with student managers to decide consequences for wrongdoer/s if they choose not to attend or to leave during the conference

☐ Meet with primary victims to seek their approval for a conference

☐ Brief victims about the questions they will be asked

☐ Meet with the wrongdoer/s to seek their agreement to go ahead with the conference, gather information from them about the incident, brief them about the conference process, in particular the questions they will be asked

☐ Choose an appropriate time of day which will allow time to convene the conference perhaps leading into a break

☐ Organise with the school managers time release for teachers attending the conference

☐ Make copies of the script, the agreement and the letter to parents (where appropriate)

☐ Allow sufficient time to familiarise yourself with the script and how it will be adapted for your circumstances

☐ Organise the classroom and seating plan

☐ If possible, organise refreshments to conclude the conference

☐ Complete the necessary paperwork for record keeping purposes

☐ Debrief with a colleague after the conference

Letter to parents

School letterhead

Date

Dear Mr and Mrs ...,

For some time now the teachers and students in class 6DM have had some concerns about the levels of disruption occurring. Students and teachers have been complaining about the loss of focus on learning because of the behaviour of several of the students, and your son Luke has been amongst this group. As you are aware from our previous conversations in meetings and phone calls, we have been trying to overcome Luke's lack of focus with a variety of strategies.

Naturally, Luke and the other students have their own stories to tell about what has been happening, so yesterday, the Student Welfare Co-ordinator, Mr Taggart, called a special meeting for the whole class to address these issues. The process used was a classroom conference, a version of Community Conferencing that this school uses to address serious behaviours which cause harm to others. Its purpose is to give all the students in the class and their teachers a voice about what has been happening, and to come to some agreement about how to make things right and ensure that these behaviours do not continue.

Participation in the conference was voluntary for everybody and it was pleasing that Luke chose to attend. It should be noted that this is an educative process and not a disciplinary or punitive one. The aim is to restore and strengthen relationships, so that the class can function in a healthy way.

I have included a copy of the agreement that this class reached yesterday for your own records. There are some obligations that Luke has been asked to meet. Luke participated satisfactorily in the conference and seems to have a better understanding now of how his inappropriate behaviour has been affecting others' as well as his own learning. We will be continuing to support Luke's learning and hope he respects the agreement the class reached. If his behaviours persist, the school will contact you requesting your participation in a community conference to deal with the matter. I have enclosed some information about the process for your interest. Contact me if you have any questions about the process we used yesterday or its outcomes, and be reassured that we have Luke's best interests at heart.

Regards,

John Brantom,
Assistant Principal

Recommended reading

There has been so much written about restorative justice and psychological theory that explains their effectiveness – texts, conference papers, research – that a beginner could be overwhelmed. What we recommend below is a starting point. Each of these publications will lead you elsewhere. Do read more. It will increase your overall understanding of the field and ultimately, your practice.

Texts

- *Crime, Shame and Reintegration.* 1989. Braithwaite, J.; Cambridge University Press.
- *Restorative Justice and Civil Society.* 2001. Ed Strang, H., and Braithwaite, J.; Cambridge University Press.
- *Queen Bees and Wannabes.* 2002. Wiseman, R; Piatkus Publishers.
- *From Surviving to Thriving.* 1998. Fuller, A.; The Australian Council for Educational Research Ltd.
- *Calling the Circle – The First and Future Culture.* 1994. Baldwin, C.; Bantam.
- *The Little Book of Restorative Justice.* Zehr, H., Mika, H.; Sage.

Articles

- The Name of the Game is Shame. Nathanson, D.L. *www.tomkins.org*
- Fundamental Concepts of Restorative Justice. Zehr, H., Mika, H. *ojp.usdoj.gov/nij/rest-just/ch1/fundamental.html*
- Restorative Justice in Everyday Life: Beyond the Formal Ritual. Wachtel, T. *Restorativepractices.org/library/anu/html*

Available from Incentive Publishing

- *Beyond Zero Tolerance: Restorative Practices in Schools* DVD. 2002–3. International Institute for Restorative Practices.
- *Conferencing Handbook.* 1999. O'Connell, T., Wachtel, B. and Wachtel, T.
- *Face to Face* DVD. 2003. Somerset Youth Offending Team.
- *Introducing Restorative Justice* DVD. 2005. Milton Keynes Psychological Service.
- *Just Schools: A Whole School Approach to Restorative Justice.* 2003. Hopkins, B.
- *Roundtable Discussion 1* DVD. International Institute for Restorative Practices.
- *Roundtable Discussion 2* DVD. International Institute for Restorative Practices.
- *Restorative Practices and Bullying: Rethinking Behaviour Management.* 2008. Thorsborne, M. and Vinegrad, D.
- *Restorative Practices in Schools: Rethinking Behaviour Management.* 2008. Thorsborne, M. and Vinegrad, D.
- *Six Conferences* DVD, International Institute for Restorative Practices.

Other useful web addresses

- *restorativepractices.org*
- *thorsborne.com.au*
- *transformingconflict.org*

Case studies

Classroom conflict in Year 8 – applying the 'no blame' conference

It was the beginning of the school year and classes had been running for ten weeks. In the staffroom, teachers were talking about how uncontrollable some classes had become. The name-calling and general noise was distracting and unbearable. Nothing seemed to work; detentions, rule reminders, phone calls to parents all seemed ineffective in curbing the disruption. Some teachers recalled when the Assistant Principal had visited a similar class and dispensed warnings to all students about their behaviour. A letter was then sent home to parents informing them about the poor behaviour of the class. In response some parents wanted their children to be placed in other classes. One teacher in particular, who was new to the school, sought some assistance from the Year Level Coordinator and the Student Welfare Coordinator. This is what happened.

The following is a transcript from the classroom teacher to the Student Welfare Coordinator and Year Level Coordinator.

Students were making masks for Carnival. Danni sat alone at a table. She was approached by Chris. Danni asked to be left alone. I asked Chris to return to her seat. Chris, Tara and Del complained that teachers were always "on Danni's side". While I was trying to sort this out, the boys on the other side of the room created increasing noise. I heard Brendan accusing Tom of racism. Earlier in the same period, Tom had deliberately cut into another student's mask, obviously trying to provoke – but no reaction came. My strong impression was that Tom was now out to provoke Brendan, who was obviously becoming distressed. Just before the sound of the bell, Brendan was so aggravated that he was about to throw a chair across the room.

Danni ran out of the room, followed by Tegan. Del, Tara and Chris urged me to sign a diary note so they could go and see the Student Welfare Coordinator. I then moved to Brendan but was unable to stop him from casting the chair across the table. Tom gave a big grin, asserting that HE had done nothing wrong. Brendan was by now so angry that I was unable to stop him from throwing the chair and leaving the room. During my lunch hour I located the Year Level Coordinator who was speaking to Danni, and I felt that I should not interrupt them. I had a

class after lunch and by the time I located the Year Level Coordinator again they had to go to a class. I had to leave school to look after my son who was home ill. Friday last period is my time off as I work part time.

P.S. I believe Brendan has been racially abused in this group before. I have heard him accuse Josh and Kris of racism on another occasion. Could Brendan be invited to give his side?

What was done?

The Student Welfare Coordinator met with the Assistant Principal and Year Level Coordinator. The note from the teacher triggered a quick review of how this class had been progressing over the past ten weeks of term. It was not good! Other teachers had made similar anecdotal comments about the class. Open defiance and aggression towards each other, long term harassment, both verbal and physical, trouble spilling into the classroom from the lockers and playground, a very challenging group of young people. It was difficult separating wrongdoers from victims, and bystanders were guilty for supporting the behaviour and not seeking help.

It was decided to conduct a classroom conference. This followed reaching agreement about what outcomes the school wanted to achieve. These included wanting teachers and students to participate in a process that could address the harm done and go some way towards resolving the conflict.

What happened at the conference?

With permission from the teacher the note was read out at the start of the conference. Students were then asked to respond and say how these incidents had affected them. Some time was then taken to explore the depth and breadth of the harm that resulted, with students telling their stories. A picture was painted of long-term harassment that some felt was 'mucking around'. Others felt so bad that they didn't want to come to school. At this point the class talked about what else had happened over the past ten weeks. Stories unfolded of awful comments and horrible put downs, harassment in the corridor and playground on a daily basis. Those teachers present used the opportunity to vent feelings of frustration and failure about teaching the class. Students apologised to each other and to their teachers without prompting. Teachers apologised to students for making little effort to prepare interesting lessons – 'It just wasn't worth the effort for such a horrible class'.

The conference moved on to make plans about the future. 'What can we do about the noise level?' Many students made suggestions that then resulted in a vote being taken on what would be tried out for two weeks. Teachers offered rewards to the class if things went well.

What's happened since?

Things settled down quickly, teachers felt that 'control' was regained. The racially abused student won his way to a student councillor's job and was voted secretary of the student council. The teachers reported unexpected experiences from the conference, almost relief about a very difficult situation to manage in a culturally diverse school. The class is now considered "normal" – just going about their business. The teacher who wrote the note has become a permanent teacher at the school and enjoys working with the class. This is the only conference that the class has experienced, yet social dynamics and relationships are OK for the moment. It could be predicted that without this conference the tensions would have remained and conflict would have flared up for the remainder of the time that these students were together at school.

Year 3 'no blame' conference

Modifying the 'no blame" conference for a primary classroom is simple. Simply take into account the age of the students and the behaviour of the class as a whole, whilst sticking to the script and keeping an eye on time.

This particular Year 3 class had a history of being disruptive and non-compliant to even the most simple of daily routines. The teachers of this grade found working with them stressful and frustrating. A no blame conference was recommended as a start to resolve some of the disharmony in the room and to put these children in a position of addressing the behaviour of some students in a supportive way and deciding the way forward for all these young people and their teachers.

The conference was planned for first thing in the morning straight after a whole school morning assembly. As these children were going to be expected to sit in a circle for a period of 30 minutes (something they usually found difficult), it was decided to have 15 minutes of physical activity to "blow off some steam". This proved to be highly beneficial and enjoyable. Once back in the

classroom, they were asked to write on a piece of paper the things that had been done to them or seen done to others that were harmful. There were no names, and being Grade 3, the statements were simple and to the point: calling me names, teasing, punching, fighting. The two part-time teachers were in attendance as well as two integration aides and the assistant principal.

The circle was organised quickly and the conference began. The statements were read out and "a talking scroll" made to be the talking piece. The rules were mentioned and agreed upon. The teachers were asked to speak first (from the heart) about how they felt about teaching this particular Grade 3 – the highs, lows and frustrations.

Using the "talking scroll" we then explored how they felt about the behaviour, how it affected them and who else had been affected. They used simple language like "bad", "awful", "it hurts", and agreed that there were many people including parents, other classes and school volunteers who had been significantly affected by the behaviour of many of the students. It was agreed by all present that things needed to change.

There were many surprises for the staff participating when it came to taking responsibility for behaviour. Disclosures like "I kicked Miss Lucy (teacher) and I'm sorry" and "I'm sorry I punched Muhammed yesterday" were heard and acknowledged.

The question "What needs to be done to make things better?" was met with lots of ideas and suggestions for making class a happier place. These were agreed upon and the conference closed. This conference took no more than 30 minutes and it was noted for this particular group that was a long time to stay engaged. The agreement was written on a large sheet of paper and displayed prominently in the room. It was discussed in impromptu class meetings and modified accordingly.

A follow-up classroom conference took place some six weeks later. The follow-up conference began with a short "circle game" to allow the students to feel at one with their classmates before beginning the hard work of the conference. It was clear to this facilitator that there had been much improvement, but there was still some way to go. Frustrations were clear when the students felt that one of their teachers wasn't following through with the agreement. The notion of collective accountability and collective responsibility and "fair process" applied to everyone!

The 'horrible' Year 7 class – a 'no blame' conference

Teachers at a large 7–12 high school reported that students in a Year 7 class were being 'horrible' to each other.

Behaviours included put downs, name calling, constant classroom noise, and comments about each other's mothers. One teacher worked with this group of students for up to seven classes each week and was at a loss as to how to stop the negative interactions and improve the worrying classroom environment. A classroom conference was suggested as a way of addressing the disturbing behaviour and also as a way to 'teach' some emotional/social skills. Student managers wished to address the harm, prevent further incidents and try to put in place some safeguards so that this would not happen again.

The conference was held in the school library with about twenty students, the librarian, a student support officer and two teachers, one taking the role of facilitator. The focus of the conference was on the verbal harassment of each other and the emotional harm that had resulted. Students were asked to talk about how they had been hurt by these comments. During the conference a student revealed that his mother had left the family only two weeks ago and that these comments about his mother were really tough to hear. Another boy spoke about the pain of his mother being diagnosed with breast cancer and how hurtful it was to be reminded of this in classes. Others talked about the class being stopped from completing their work and feelings of frustration and anger at the put downs and teasing. One teacher spoke about feelings of personal failure, having been responsible for putting together a one day anti-harassment programme for all students in Year 7 which had clearly not worked.

Students were asked to talk about who had been affected by their behaviour. As people were identified, the students were then asked in what ways they had been affected. Students realised that future Year 7 camps might not go ahead because of their behaviour; teachers might be reluctant to go again as much of the verbal harassment had begun at this year's camp held just a few months earlier. Some students were surprised to hear that so many people were impacted upon by what had happened.

Then it was time to go around the circle and ask the 'perpetrators' to acknowledge what they had done.

They were told that what they said would go no further and no one would be punished, but their comments would go some way to making things better. To their credit many students admitted to their behaviour and the harm that they were responsible for. Without prompting many apologised to the class and gave guarantees that this would not happen again. Students began to sit upright in their chairs, heads were slowly raised and eye contact with each other became possible. One student participated for most of the conference with his head held in his hands staring down at the ground. The worst attacks had been on him, with comments of 'gay' and 'faggot' reducing him to a state of deep shame and helplessness. Toward the end of the conference this student raised his head and made eye contact with the perpetrators. The conference had gone some way to healing the wounds.

Since this conference things have been much better. The teasing and harassment that prompted this response has not surfaced again. Of significance are the protective behaviours of the class since this conference. They request a conference before things get out of hand and sense when tensions develop and relationships are strained. Of course the normal adolescent conflict and social squabbles happen but they now use a better way to resolve and talk through trouble. For the school this was the first no blame conference. It was the start of something good that gave us a way to work 'with' disruptive classes as opposed to doing things 'to' students.

The literacy camp: conferencing for off-campus activities

A school planned to take a group of thirteen Year 7 students on a 'literacy camp' to the local university for a five-day programme.

The idea was to provide intensive literacy support each morning and in the afternoon use a range of recreational and sporting venues close to the university as a means of developing the social and personal skills of the students. Experience had shown that most students with very low literacy levels (many of these students did not even register on common reading and comprehension tests) usually present with challenging behaviours. The hypothesis underpinning this camp was that by using a range of intensive strategies, it would be possible to improve the reading age by many months (if not years) over the five-day period of the camp.

These students had also participated in other literacy programmes throughout the year and teachers running this camp were concerned about the potential anti-social and negative behaviour that would need some 'strong' management. Teachers knew all too well the problems that might be encountered and the school was glad to be free of these particular students for a whole week.

The education faculty at the university was keen to get involved and provided several undergraduate students to act as mentors. It was surprising to discover that this was the first adolescent group he faculty had worked with on campus for over ten years.

It was agreed that by the end of the week teachers would be exhausted and frustrated if an authoritarian and punitive approach was taken to managing student behaviour. Instead, a restorative approach was adopted to build in some protective strategies and respond to incidents of misconduct as they occurred. Each morning before work began, a classroom conference was conducted with all students. Explicit statements were made about what the day would involve and what behaviours were expected from everybody. Students were then asked what the teachers could do to help them get through the day and achieve what was planned. A key moment in each of the morning conferences was to ask what things needed to be resolved from the previous day. The short bus trip from school to the university was enough opportunity for tensions to build within the group: "You took my seat", "She stuck her finger up at my sister when we went past my house!", "Who took my crisp packet?" A significant theme that continually needed to be addressed was the high level of 'bitchiness' between female students. The boys would then use the conflict to provoke the girls with rumours and lies. These squabbles and rumours would have driven teachers quite mad if a punitive approach was taken. Threats of sending students back to school, contacting parents, banning them from activities would just address the symptoms, not the cause. So, each time trouble was reported or detected, the programme stopped and an appropriate conference was facilitated.

Individual and small group conferences were held away from the main group and at other times the whole group were called together. The choice of conference size depended on who had what done to them and by whom. Three days into the camp students began asking for a 'conference' to sort out

their differences with each other. A significant change came over the group in the way they wanted to resolve conflict.

So what was the key to the success of using these restorative processes? The morning conference gave students clear messages and information about what was planned for the day. This meant that they felt safe and secure about what was expected of them and what they needed to do, where to be, and how long for. Also, it allowed students a forum where their concerns could be heard, and more importantly, addressed. The success of the individual and small group conferences rested on the use of the simple script and the avoidance of lecturing and threatening the group. Of significance were the feelings of teachers at the end of the camp. All felt relaxed from spending a week without the stress of trying to 'control' student behaviour through sanctions and warnings, and there was a sense of pride in seeing real improvement in student social skills and emotional literacy. Reading ages improved as well!

'Muck up day' – a large group conference

It is tradition and practice in some Australian and other Western schools for students in the final year of their high school life to celebrate the last day of school with some light hearted, often outrageous and sometimes reckless behaviour.

'Muck up Day' or 'Schoolies Week' is a symbolic ritual bringing closure to an intense period of growth and separation from significant others. Celebrations may involve some harmless pranks including egg throwing, flour or water bomb fights, parades or theatrical performances. It may be a single day of celebration or a whole week of tricks and parties. In the extreme, it sometimes involves terrorising the younger members of the school community, acts of property damage and physical assault. Sometimes young adults not connected with any school join in, causing school administrators to employ security guards and other measures that often add to the tensions and increase the temperature.

At one school, 'Muck up Day' went wrong. The day involved a collection of incidents both at school and in the local community. 'Muck up Day' was planned for Year 12 students but some Year 11 students joined in and this is when the problems began. One Year 11 student truanted from school and joined a group of young adults who roamed the neighbourhood wearing black balaclavas. Many of these local residents had come to the area as migrants and refugees with chilling memories of terror and trauma from their homelands. The balaclavas caused great distress and refreshed some terrible memories. Several other Year 11 students ambushed junior students with eggs – so many eggs that in one case, a student carried his loaded into a shopping trolley. Two other Year 11 students joined in the flour and water bomb battle between mobs on the school oval. The action on the oval spilled over to affect several teachers who felt threatened and targeted by the unruly mob. The school had instructed all Year 11 students to be in their classrooms for the day and to keep away from the celebrations.

The school was deeply concerned about the events that day. Despite a great deal of negotiation and compromise everybody felt let down by senior students. Some felt that all future 'Muck up Days' should be banned and that trust and safety had been lost altogether. 'Muck up Day' had come to cause fear in the school community each year. Some teachers would not bring their cars to school fearing retribution for past conflicts with students. Parents of junior students would keep their children home for the day as a protective measure.

Other staff felt that a different response was needed. A conference with all Year 11 students was suggested as a way to address and resolve the issues that caused harm to the school community. The school principal was new to the job and agreed that a conference would be helpful in beginning a culture change amongst the Year 11 student body. Teachers, administrators and about one hundred Year 11 students met in the performing arts studio for the conference. Before the conference was organised the wrongdoers were given the option of participating with the group to hear how others felt about what happened that day and what needed to be done to fix things up, or having their actions managed differently by the school. All but one of these students chose to attend the conference. This student had a history of wrongdoing, including encouraging team mates to 'throw' a soccer game so that a rival school would not reach the finals. Once again he failed to accept any responsibility for his behaviour. As a result a meeting with parents and student administrators was organised resulting in his exclusion from any future celebrations of his year level.

Several teachers and key students addressed the group about why they had been called together. Stories were told so that everybody understood what had occurred on 'Muck up Day'. Prior to this, rumours around the school were doing little to help restore relationships and address concerns. Students were divided into groups of eight and each group received a worksheet with some questions to discuss. Teachers moved around and assisted each group as needed. Groups were asked to appoint a spokesperson and after about thirty minutes of discussion, feedback was gathered. Each spokesperson came to the front of the studio and responded to some of these questions. Time did not allow the group to respond to all questions.

Questions to each group:

How do you feel about what has happened?

What impact has this incident had on you and others?

What has been the hardest thing for you?

What would you like to see happen to right the wrongs?

What would a good outcome look like from this conference?

The wrongdoers were taken aside when the groups got down to work. They were asked to reflect on some questions and make their responses public before the main group. They were asked if they were also prepared to answer any questions that the group might have.

Questions to the wrongdoers:

How did you get involved and what happened?

What were you thinking/feeling at the time this happened?

What have you thought about since this happened?

Who has been affected by what you did?

What can you do to repair the harm?

Students who spoke on behalf of their group all rejected the behaviours of the wrongdoers. Most said that everybody was surprised by what the boys had done, it was out of character. The wrongdoers offered apologies and guarantees about future behaviour. One boy wrote a very moving letter of apology that was posted on the common room notice board the next day. The group asked the wrongdoer who used the balaclava to write an apology in the community newsletter hoping that those affected would read it. Teachers present were impressed and, more importantly, felt reassured by the maturity and responsibility shown by the group.

Some questions and comments made by the group to the wrongdoers:

Do you know that what you did may mean that our 'Muck

up day' next year could be cancelled?

People now think that we are all bad people because of what you did.

You had no right to do this!

No one trusts us now, how do we fix that?

The Year 12s met with the Principal to work out what would be OK for the day and you guys went and did this.

The next stage of the conference focused on the future and putting in place safeguards for the school and community. Before the conference, administrators agreed that an ideal outcome would be to stimulate a culture change amongst the students. The plan was to read out some set questions and ask students to respond randomly.

Questions to everybody at the conference:

What do you think needs to change to reduce the tensions about 'Muck up Day' and allow everyone including teachers and students to enjoy this day?

Can we change the name of the day to promote more positive behaviour from everybody?

In what other ways can we celebrate our last day and prevent harm to people?

There was not enough time to explore these questions so the group were asked to write down their responses, which would be collected over the next few days. It was promised to post these up in the common room for all to see. Since this conference the name has changed from 'Muck up Day' to 'Celebration Day' and students are planning a food feast well away from the school in a local park.

 ### Case management for 'difficult' students

Many schools have a population of students who exist on the periphery of mainstream classes and carry a range of labels: school refusers, recalcitrants, sub-culture, drop outs, etc.

The case management of these students may involve a range of teachers and support staff meeting regularly to review and put in place modified programmes. These meetings are ideal opportunities for the restorative script to be used as dialogue and to guide discussion. Progress and/or "back-sliding" can be discussed in a way that preserves dignity and focuses on the impact on relationships.

Susan is present at her case management meeting with her mother. Susan is in year 9 and has a history of broken homes and interrupted schooling. Others at the meeting include social worker, support teacher, student administrator and a welfare teacher. The meeting is one of the regular monthly meetings to monitor progress and provide support.

Susan and her mother are asked the following 'scripted' questions:

Tell us how the past month has been. What has happened?

Susan and her mother report some real progress. Attendance at school has increased and her class work is showing some real improvement.

Susan, what were you thinking about when you came to school the last few weeks and did some work?

Susan says that it so boring at home and the shopping mall is not safe any more. Some of the work in class was easy.

How do you feel about what you have achieved?

Susan: *Good. Mum is off my back for a change!*

What have you thought about since you have been working well and coming to school?

Susan: *I suppose that I'm lucky to still have a chance. My friends want me to come to school.*

Susan, who is affected by your behaviour when you attend school and work well? How about your mum?

Susan's mum: *She is less stressed and we have stopped fighting.*

Who else is affected? How about you?

Susan: *Sometimes I feel happy that I am doing what my friends are doing. I am good at art.*

How are some of the people at this meeting affected by your positive progress? Let's find out. We will go around the room and see how people feel.

The case management meeting continues with participants offering positive comments about the impact of Susan's improved behaviour. What we seek to achieve from this process is a focus on the social and relational meaning of Susan's behaviour in an effort to build on relationships with significant people in her life. Ideally we hope that the process can encourage and teach young people to move from thoughts of 'self' to consideration of 'others'.

About the authors

Margaret Thorsborne

Margaret has a long history in education, guidance and counselling. Her passion while employed in education had always been to find better ways to build and rebuild relationships between teachers, students and other members of the school community, to enhance teaching and learning outcomes. She and like-minded colleagues were therefore keen to discover more effective interventions to deal with those sorts of incidents in schools such as bullying, abuse, conflict and violence which did not respond positively to traditional punitive sanctions. She was, therefore, inspired by stories of conferencing, then being used in justice agencies. Always a risk-taker, Margaret convened the first ever school-based conference with a little telephone coaching from a police officer, and has never looked back! She managed a ground breaking pilot of community conferencing in her educational region, and is now consultant to a number of government education departments in Australia and abroad wishing to change the policy, practice and culture of behaviour management in schools. Now a private consultant, she continues to work in schools as well as in private and public sector workplaces, convening conferences for high level conflict and inappropriate behaviour and providing training in conference facilitation for middle and senior management.

David Vinegrad

David is a veteran of working in a diversity of school settings and undertaking a wide range of roles in classroom teaching, student counselling and management. His work experience covers several states of Australia and he is now involved in International Schooling in Japan. His interest in Restorative Justice stemmed from a concern about the use of traditional school-based measures when wrongdoing occurred. Student behaviour did not change, much conflict remained unresolved and the chance to promote positive teacher–student relationships was often lost. David was greatly encouraged when he undertook some professional development in Restorative Justice and has since become an innovative leader in classroom approaches. After doing some pioneering work in Tasmania with like-minded educators and police he moved to Victoria to continue spreading the word. At the time of writing David is working 'restoratively' in classrooms with his students as well as acting as consultant to the Ministry of Education Singapore and a number of International schools in Japan.

Other titles on Restorative Practices by Margaret Thorsborne & David Vinegrad

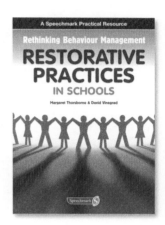

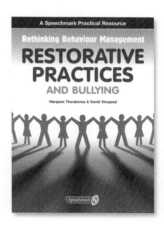

Restorative Practices in Schools

This essential title includes the following:

- How to analyse the whole current school practice
- Detailed guidance on organising a 'Community Conference'
- Frequently asked questions and answers
- Case studies.

Restorative Practices and Bullying

The authors offer a useful guide to dealing with this difficult subject:

- Restorative justice and behaviour management
- An explanation of the restorative practice approach to bullying
- Detailed descriptions of restorative responses to bullying incidents
- Frequently asked questions and answers
- Case studies.